ISLAM
Plain and Simple

TARIQ JALIL

Islam Plain and Simple
Women, Terrorism, and Other Controversial Topics

Published by Quinn Press™
Santa Monica, CA

Library of Congress Control Number: 2013915516

Jalil, Tariq, Author
Islam Plain and Simple: Women, Terrorism,
and Other Controversial Topics
Tariq Jalil

ISBN 978-0-615-7975-6
1. Religion
2. Islam

This book has been endorsed by the following:

Dr. Eboo Patel – Adviser to the White House

Professor Michael Morony – UCLA, History Department,
Islamic Studies Program Chair

Professor Akbar Ahmed ¬– American University,
Chair of Islamic Studies

Professor Juan Cole – University of Michigan,
History Department, Commentator,
Author of *Engaging the Muslim World*

Dr. Reza Aslan – Author of the international bestseller
No god but God and *How to Win a Cosmic War,*
Commentator on the Daily Beast

ACKNOWLEDGMENTS

Mazhar, Betty, Arshia, Ilham, Carol, Maura, Anna, Munir, Polly, James, all the endorsers, and everyone who took the time to make sure this book is accurate and not a complete bore.

ISLAM
Plain and Simple

WOMEN, TERRORISM, AND
OTHER CONTROVERSIAL TOPICS

TARIQ JALIL

CONTENTS

INTRODUCTION

This book has been written for the sole purpose of informing the reader about the foundational beliefs of a religion that is followed by approximately 1.6 billion people. Great lengths have been taken to provide complete and factual information with every major topic and sub-topic referenced by a reliable source.

Unfortunately, in the modern day, a reasoned and unbiased examination of Islam is becoming difficult. Newscasts often show only violent images of Muslims while certain organizations and political parties have used Islam as a scapegoat for all the world's ills. While Muslim extremists undoubtedly exist and undoubtedly commit acts of violence and oppression, these people only comprise a small minority of Islam's followers, and like most extremists, are the least qualified to represent their religion's principles and teachings.

Also working against Islam's image is the common misperception that countries with Muslim majorities are backwards politically, economically and socially. While this is true in some cases, there are many countries like Turkey, Bangladesh, and Indonesia that represent some of the fastest growing economies in the world. Many people in the West do not consider these countries when discussing Islam because most people believe the Arab Middle East is the sole representative of the religion. However, all the Arab countries put together only comprise about 15% of the Muslim World.

The intent of this book is to correct misconceptions in order to explain the fundamentals of Islam in a simple and factual way. It will also attempt to address its most controversial topics. Again, the information contained within has been meticulously annotated in order to show that the Islamic principles presented are absolutely verifiable within its texts. This book is a basic overview and not meant to be exhaustive; however, reading this book in its entirety should give one an accurate overview of traditional Islam, with the complexities and vagaries of history that followed the death of Muhammad removed. It is the author's hope that by examining the fundamentals of the religion, light can be shed on those beliefs and practices that Muslims have believed, and perhaps, in some cases, should return to. At its heart, Islam is a simple faith that allows its followers to embrace a level of devotion and commitment that suits the needs and inclinations of the individuals who follow its message. Despite the unfair reputation that the faith has earned in recent times, readers will hopefully come away from this text with a more complete understanding of a faith that has helped change the shape of the world.

A NOTE ON SOURCES:

A great deal of effort has been made to integrate specific references to the Quran and the most broadly accepted of the various Hadith. Through this, it is hoped that the faith of Islam and the words of the Prophet Muhammad will be permitted to speak for themselves. I have followed the standard reference method for identifying passages from the Quran; specifically, Sura (or chapter) and Verse separated by a colon. I have relied on the Muhammad Asad English translation, available in searchable form at www.islamicity.com, for my translations of Quranic verses.

I have also included references to several major Hadith collections: the Sahih Bukhari, Sahih Muslim, the Abu Dawud, and the Shama-il Tirmidhi. These are generally considered the most authentic collections and are those that have been shown to best represent the spirit of the Quran and the person of Muhammad.

CHAPTER 1

SCIENCE AND DISCOVERY

Islam is a religion based on the belief in one God. To the Muslim, this belief cannot be accepted blindly and without question. Men and women are expected to use their intellect and the evidence around them to come to this conclusion. One is meant to ponder the existence of God, religion, and one's place in the universe, in that order. If these concepts remain unexamined, the very foundation of belief is considered weak and without merit. The Quran, the Islamic holy book, constantly asks its reader to look around them for signs of God's existence (3:190, 2:118) and to examine everything within the universe for meaning.

Muslim scientists point to DNA and molecular structure as coded building blocks that make up everything in the Universe. Nothing in nature, they say, is completely chaotic; everything is built with a scientific code that is governed by a law. This observation may then lead one to deduce that such precise structure and laws might have been planned in a deliberate and intelligent way, which could mean these things were created by something sentient—a god. The Quran encourages one to study nature and science to find signs of God's existence. In other words, in Islam, science is evidence of God's existence, not proof against him.

The Quran constantly asks its readers to view the earth as an epiphany: Muslims are to use their reason and intelligence to find evidence for God's existence in the world around them. The Quran reads:

> Verily, in the creation of the heavens and of the earth, and the succession of night and day: and in the ships that speed through the sea with what is useful to man: and in the waters which God sends down from the sky, giving life thereby to the earth after it had, been lifeless, and causing all manner of living creatures to multiply thereon: and in the change of the winds, and the clouds that run their appointed courses between sky and earth: [in all this] there are messages indeed for people who use their reason (2:164).

It's important to note that devotion to human reason is encouraged in Islam. Exploration of the world, its inhabitants, and the scientific laws that rule it reinforce what Muslims have been taught about God. It is this spirit of exploration that inspired the Muslims of the 8th–14th centuries to make such advances in the study of algebra, geometry, and trigonometry. They were also instrumental in developing many aspects of modern medicine and the type of critical analysis known as "the scientific method."

In more modern times, Muslim scientists have pointed to verses in the Quran that make accurate, modern scientific observations. For instance, chapter 86 refers to a piercing, knocking star, the description of which corresponds to the then-unknown celestial body today called a pulsar. It is from examples like this that Muslims welcome scientific revelation. For instance, many educated Muslims believe in the "Big Bang Theory" and its resulting phenomenon and would only argue about what started or incited creation — namely, God. Many scientists have written entire volumes on the Quran[1], Islam and Science that cannot be covered in a book such as this. However, the point remains that Islam does not ask its followers to dismiss science in lieu of religious teaching but rather encourages discovery of religion through science.

Along these lines, Muslims are encouraged to study nature and history in order to recognize God's signs and to understand His will. In Islam, it's not just religious scholars who are held in high regard, but also scientists, academic scholars, or any person who spends time studying and examining a particular subject. This is because such people are not only gaining knowledge in their field, but by doing so, they're also attempting to understand God's nature and intention.

If one's own reason does lead to belief in the existence of God, Islam then asks its followers to consider the laws of the universe—physics, biology, and chemistry—all the laws that keep the world in a state of harmony and equilibrium (32:7, 95:4). Again, one is

---

1. One of the other purported miracles of the Quran is that it can be memorized word for word. There are a good numbers of Muslims who have memorized all 77,701 words in sequence.

asked to reason that if God established these laws for everything in the universe, then it is reasonable to conclude that God established laws for humanity as well. Following these laws should help an individual attain harmony with God's will and, in turn, with oneself—physically, mentally, and spiritually. In effect, they enable an individual to achieve equilibrium.

The word *islam* in the Arabic language means "peace," "submission," and "purity." So a follower of Islam, a Muslim (capitalized), is an individual who submits to the laws of God as revealed in the Quran. When the "m" in *muslim* is not capitalized, the word refers to anyone or anything that submits to the will of God. Therefore, in Arabic, the setting sun is "muslim" in the sense that it must obey God's law of physics. A human is born "muslim," as it's born from a state of peace. Muslims believe that when humans veer away from God's teachings, they go against their own natural inclination towards God's laws. The inference is if one does follow these teachings, they should lead back to a state of peace and harmony. If one doesn't, it can lead to disharmony in one's life. In Islam, religion must be applicable and beneficial in one's daily life, as that is one of its main purposes. It is God's teachings that hold the secrets to life, secrets that will lead to a better-balanced physical and spiritual existence.

Along these lines, Islam is also careful to point out that ignoring God's laws can lead to discord and detract from one's sense of inner peace. Distractions like career or wealth (not that either are evil within themselves) can cause a person to live an entire life without bothering to address life's meaning. Not attending to spirituality, or worse, purposely going *against* God's laws, can lead to a lack of inner peace (70:19). This can then become a contributing factor to a sort of depression (113:3). In extreme cases, a lack of inner peace can lead to reckless or self-destructive behavior.

It's important to note that in Islam, God is mainly referred to as "Allah" (pronounced like 'a lot' without the 't') or *The* God. This is an Arabic word used not only by Muslims, but by Arab Christians in Bethlehem and across the Middle East. Allah is considered to be an all-knowing Creator and is the same God of the Jews and Christians—the God of Moses and Abraham (2:124). Islam, however, teaches that God has no sons or daughters (112:3), or any partners (6:22–24): "Your God is the One God, there is no deity save He" (2:163). He is neither distinctly male nor female, (even though 'He' or the royal 'We' is used when quoting Him). He is most often described in the Quran as the most Merciful and the most Compassionate – attributes that refer to the statement that He loves humanity (3:76) and sustains, rewards, and protects His followers.

LIFE AND DEATH

Muslims consider life in this world to be only a tiny part of an eternal timeline—a small spot on a long line that stretches to infinity. The Quran states that death is inevitable, yet despite all scholarly arguments concerning God and religion, no person knows what happens after death (28:88, 62:8). It then asserts that there is indeed life after death, and each individual will earn reward or punishment based on actions in this life (28:85). The Quran does not subscribe to the notion that everything in life is wicked and sinful, nor does it believe life should be work-free or dedicated to pleasure. Rather, Islam intends to help followers identify a moderate path, as well as life's meaning and purpose. In this vein, the Quran stresses that while life after death is the ultimate destination, one should not completely ignore the responsibilities and joys of this life (17:18–17:21).

Islam views life as a test, a test to see whether one will follow God's teachings or be distracted by the mundane world (18:7). According to the Quran, this is the meaning of life: to worship God despite all distractions (51:56–8). In return, God will provide worldly sustenance and inner peace, as well as reward in the next life. Accordingly, God assures each individual that no one will be given more burdens than they can bear (2:286). The Quran goes on to state that people who bear pain and suffering in this world will be rewarded for it in the next life, and their painful memories removed (7:42–43).

THE DAY OF JUDGMENT

Islam teaches that the world will come to an end at some point. No one knows when this will happen except God. The Quran states that on this day, "Each will stand alone and naked before God as judge" (35:18). This means that no one will be responsible for the actions of another (82:19), and everything a person has done will be revealed in the presence of God and he/she will be judged accordingly.

CHAPTER 2

THE ORIGINAL MESSAGE

I slam constantly reminds its followers that it is the original religion given to humanity at the beginning of human existence and continually renewed. This message of God's existence and Oneness, coupled with guidelines for living, has been given to every generation of humankind through a prophet or messenger. Each time people started to stray from God's religion, a human messenger was sent to remind them of God's consistent message. The process started with Adam and continued with subsequent messengers like Abraham, Noah, Moses, and Jesus (2:136, 4:163–165)[1]. To the Muslim, the message brought by Mohammed does not overturn the revelations given to the *original* Christians and

1. The role of Jesus in Islam will be explained in the following chapter.

Jews. However, it is important to note that Muslims believe that some of these original revelations have now changed since the beginnings of Christianity and Judaism. To Muslims, Islam is the pure, final, and ultimate word of God to His creation.

Previous messengers of God were all considered blessed, but ultimately still human; a belief that has created some theological friction between adherents to Islam and their Christian counterparts. The Quran describes different messengers as having been fallible (38:24–25) and victims of self-doubt (28:33–35). Some even acted rashly (28:14–21) and needed to seek God's guidance and forgiveness (7:151). This human frailty was displayed precisely to show their followers that the messengers *were* human and therefore relatable—real human examples to live up to. Perfect humans would be impossible to relate to or emulate—only God is perfect and, therefore, the *only* being worthy of worship.

In Islam, all of the prophets like Abraham and Moses taught God's one true religion and are considered muslim: people who submitted and attained peace through God and his laws. The Quran reads:

> And indeed, within every community have We raised up an apostle [entrusted with this message]: "Worship God, and shun false gods." And among those [past generations] were people whom God graced with His guidance, just as there were among them [many] who inevitably fell prey to grievous error: go, then, about the earth and behold what happened in the end to those who gave the lie to the truth (16:36).

Some Islamic scholars suggest that a variety of religious teachers like Buddha may have been muslim, a teacher or messenger of the one true religion. Of the twenty-five prophets mentioned in the Quran, twenty-one are mentioned in the Bible. However, according to Islam, when Moses brought the One Religion to a particular group of Jews, they changed this universal message and made it a religion only for themselves. This disagreement over the role of Judaism in the history of revelation has had far-reaching implications. The current conflict over the territories of modern Israel and Palestine has some roots in this debate. Many modern day Israelis claim the land belonged to Moses and his followers. Muslims agree, but pronounce that Moses and his original followers, who were Jews racially, were literal *muslims* and therefore brothers and sisters of modern day Muslims. Along these lines, all Muslims believe Moses simply preached the One True Religion that Jesus and Muhammad taught after him- the religion that is now referred to as Islam.

Along the same lines, Jesus was said to have taught the One Religion but some of his followers changed it, worshipping Jesus himself instead of the One True God [2]. Though these differences are large, it's important to note that the Quran does not write off Judaism or Christianity:

"[But] they are not all alike: among the followers of earlier revelation there are upright people, who recite God's messages throughout the night, and prostrate themselves

---

2. The claim that Jesus is God and not a prophet was actually debated among Christians for the first 300 years of Christianity until the Council of Nicaea declared Jesus was God in 325.

[before Him]. They believe in God and the Last Day, and enjoin the doing of what is right and forbid the doing of what is wrong, and vie with one another in doing good works: and these are among the righteous (3:113-114)."

While this Quranic verse approved of the above-mentioned Christians, Muslims still believe they had erred in worshipping the prophet Jesus. That is why, 670 years after Jesus Christ was born, a new prophet came to revive the original message of the one true God. This Prophet was to bring the original message back to humanity, and his name was Muhammad.

For Muslims, Muhammad ibn Abdallah was the last of all messengers, the only and final prophet to come after Jesus. It was Muhammad who related the final teachings and commandments of God to mankind. This is why he holds such a prominent role in the religion. In fact, Muslims use almost exclusively the Quran and the teachings of Muhammad's life (known to Muslims as the Hadith) as the basis for their religion. An entire textual science has been dedicated to the Hadith alone. This science rates the Hadith to varying levels of authenticity and also interprets them in a religious and historical context.

The Quran is studied and written about even more, and is thought to be comprehended in four different ways: its literal interpretation, its symbolic interpretation, its historical context and, according to some scholars, the Quran can address one directly whereby the lessons and imperatives specifically relate to the individual reader's life.

JESUS IN ISLAM

The Quran mentions Jesus a total of n[...]
times than Muhammad. In it, he is con[...]
(5:46–47), who was sent to sent to d[...]
just as the prophets before him had si[...]
Because Jesus delivered that message and submitted to God's laws,
he is considered muslim and an example for all Muslims to follow.
The Quran also states that Jesus foretold the coming of a Messenger after himself—Muhammad (61:6). Some Muslim scholars
believe that Muhammad is mentioned in the bible[3].

The Quran specifically addresses the birth and life of Jesus
(3:35–47 and 19:16–35). It describes how Mary was given word
that she would deliver a child, who would be a great prophet.
Although a virgin, she is told that God can will anything into existence by just uttering the command, "Be," and so it is (2:117).

While this makes Jesus' birth unprecedented, Muslims do
not believe it makes Jesus the Son of God. To the Muslim, Jesus,
though very important, was still a human and was only a son of
God in the sense that all humans are considered, philosophically,
to be children of God as stated in the bible[4]. This returns to the Islamic belief that *human* prophets were always sent to deliver God's
message in order to provide a human example of how one can live.
This was considered important as people needed to know by way

---

3. Some Muslim scholars have said that "the Comforter" mentioned in the Gospel
of John (14:26, 15:26, 16:8,13–15) refers to the coming of Muhammad and that
verses in Deuteronomy (18:15,18) refer to him as well.

4. "So in Christ Jesus you are all children of God through faith (Galations 3:26),"
"Behold, what manner of love the Father hath bestowed upon us, that we should be
called the sons of God…. (John 3:1)"

example that the way of life God prescribes is actually ... to live. More importantly, it's believed that God is too ... at to become a human or has any need to portray himself in human form.

The Quran very plainly states that God creates life and is far too remote in His glory to have a son (4:171). For this reason, Jesus is often referred to in the Quran as "Jesus, son of Mary." Despite this distinction, the descriptions of Jesus' actions stand close to those described in the Bible with some exceptions. Muslims believe that Jesus was strengthened with a Divine Spirit. In the Quran, this spirit is interpreted to mean the Angel Gabriel, who would relay messages to Jesus from God. Jesus is also described as having performed miracles, such as healing the sick. However, the Quran specifically points out that these types of miracles are only delivered by God's permission and not by the individual will of the man himself (6:109). This is, again, to emphasize Jesus' human nature as contrasted against God's divinity.

The Quran also states that Jesus was dictated a book called the Injeel (5:46), but it was destroyed over time, and that the current Bible is not divinely inspired. It is also believed that the modern-day text has been changed countless times and may have lost some of its accuracy. Another very important distinction between Islam and Christianity is the concept of the crucifixion and resurrection. A verse in the Quran states that Jesus was not killed by crucifixion, but was instead "taken up" by God:

> And their boast, "Behold, we have slain the Christ Jesus, son of Mary, [who claimed to be] an apostle of God!"
> However, they did not slay him, and neither did they cru-

cify him, but it only seemed to them [as if it had been] (4:157) . . .

Despite these differences with Christianity, Jesus is still a respected and holy figure in Islam. In fact, Muslims believe that Jesus, The Messiah, will return to earth to lead people in the name of God and Islam at the end of Earth's time (43:61–68).

HUMANS' RELATION TO GOD

There is no central leader in Islam analogous to the Pope in Catholicism. In fact, there is no sanctioned clergy or priesthood either. This fact has created a unique environment within the Muslim community where the interpretation of religious texts and practice is concerned. Instead, knowledgeable leaders in the community are called *Imams* (pronounced *Eemaams*), who often give their opinion on certain religious matters. These people are asked to show the logic behind their reasoning and its basis in the religious texts. Most Muslims are encouraged to follow what scholars have determined on major matters (significant rituals, core beliefs etc.), but in minor matters, these opinions are not considered the final word and there other, equally valid positions may be reached through discussion and ongoing debate. Consequently, the individual Muslim is free to accept or reject the edicts of the Imams by virtue of his/her own reasoning. This freedom of interpretation often grants the same benefits and difficulties for a Muslim community as does the freedom of choice found within a pluralistic democracy. As such, there are conservative, liberal, literal, or allegorical interpretations of certain texts and judgments that can change from one Muslim to another. So-called "Authoritarian" or "Fundamentalist" versions of Islam are a contradiction in terms. Even in Muhammad's time, people were allowed minor differences in practice and varying levels of faith and participation.

Nevertheless, the reliance on scripture and jurisprudence are important in Islam as God does not "talk" directly to his followers except through the Quran. To the Muslim, God may give signs regarding any number of things but He does not give out new commandments or singular instructions to any individual. This is an essential aspect of Islam, as it prevents any individual from claiming an absolute understanding of God's will. It further eliminates the ability of people to create new religious edicts or claim to know how God will judge an individual after death. Since Muslims are forced to derive all of God's commandments from the same book, scholarly debate has to take place within certain boundaries and without claims of divine knowledge. It is important to note that this has not stopped some errant individuals from attempting to make such claims.

While there is an emphasis on text and reasoning, God's relation to humans is defined as a loving and close one in the Quran:

> It is We who have created man, and We know what his innermost self whispers within him: for We are closer to him than his jugular vein (50:16)[5].

This verse is often interpreted as meaning that God is always aware of a person's actions and thoughts. In Islam, God's love and

---

5. The "We," is a kind of royal "we," which in the Quran, is sometimes used by God as a more intimate form of the first person.

help is always available to an individual and to humankind in general. However, one receives more benefits when following God's laws and staying conscious of Him. It is these things that endear a person to Him:

> Nay, but [God is aware of] those who keep their bond with Him, and are conscious of Him: and, verily, God loves those who are conscious of Him (3:76).

This Divine–human relationship is intensified by an individual's effort. If one strives to attain God's favor, God responds in kind. One passage in the Hadith states that,

> Muhammad said, "My Lord says, 'If My servant comes nearer to Me for an inch, I go nearer to him a hands width; and if he comes nearer to Me a hands width, I go nearer to him for the span of outstretched arms; and if he comes to Me walking, I go to him running.' (Sahih Bukhari – 009.093.627)"

This Hadith is meant to explain the concept that if a person puts even a little effort to getting close to God, then God will multiply that effort by coming closer to him/her. Islam teaches that this closeness will result in peace of mind, an alleviation of tribulations and clear guidance for everyday decisions. It is also acknowledged that humans will inevitably stray from God's way, and that part of being a Muslim is being vigilant about coming back to Him and then, getting closer. This is done first by making the intent and then taking *actions* that God finds pleasing. If this is accomplished through one's lifetime, the Quran states that the ultimate reward comes after death, when all humans will ultimately be accountable for their actions on earth. If they are judged favorably, they will be rewarded beyond measure (6:94).

HEAVEN AND HELL

The reward is Heaven and the punishment, Hell. However, it is important to note that while there is an emphasis in the Quran on reward and mercy, there are also recommendations for punishment regarding certain deeds and actions, which will be discussed in ensuing chapters.

The descriptions of Heaven and Hell are varied in the Quran and The Hadith. In the Quran, the descriptions are mostly allegorical. For instance:

> But those who attain to faith and do righteous deeds—[and] We do not burden any human being with more than he is well able to bear—they are destined for paradise, therein to abide, after We shall have removed whatever unworthy thoughts or feelings may have been [lingering] in their bosoms. Running waters will flow at their feet (7:42–43). . .

Here, it's made clear that righteous deeds are the gateway to Heaven, and that all feelings of envy, hatred, shame, embarrassment, pain, or sorrow will be removed. The only physical description, however, is limited to the idea that "running waters will flow at their feet." This description, not necessarily meant to be taken literally but allegorically, refers to an abundance of blessings, which will be readily available. Heaven is often described as a place where each individual will have what he or she desires and where there will be total peace and rest. It is taught that, after a life of hard work in this world, one will rest and be taken care of in the next.

Hell is given the same allegorical treatment. Fire (4:145) is among the metaphors used to describe it:

> And [thus it is:] every arrogant enemy of the truth shall be undone [in the life to come], with hell awaiting him; and he shall be made to drink of the water of most bitter distress (14:15–16). . .

The "Water of bitter distress" is meant to convey the feeling one will have after a life of wronging one's self and others. The Quran constantly refers to life as a limited time to do good deeds and to repent for the bad. Once time runs out, it's too late to do either.

Lastly, in Islam, there are different levels of reward in Heaven or punishment in Hell. Ones actions would result in greater reward or more severe punishment depending on what the individual did in life. The Quran states that the judgment will be fair:

> …Brief is the enjoyment of this world, whereas the life to come is the best for all who are conscious of God - since none of you shall be wronged by as much as a hair's breadth (4:77).

ACTION VERSUS BELIEF

Islam teaches its followers that each person is born without sin and inclined toward good — a muslim. It is a person's choices in his or her adult life, which will lead them to continue toward good or lead them in the other direction. The choices made in life will determine that person's fate. Islam frequently tells its followers that faith alone is not enough and that action and practice are part of belief (Sahih Bukhari 009.093.645). As this suggests, children are exempt from judgment, and are not considered to be responsible for their salvation until reaching puberty.

While belief in God and the divine message is an important part of one's faith, it is a person's actions that are considered the ultimate expression of belief and submission. In fact, all five of Islam's basic tenets are calls to action: saying the declaration of faith, prayer, fasting, giving of charity, and the pilgrimage to Mecca. Most other tenets are also action-based, such as helping orphans and providing for one's family. This is because Islam states that belief alone is not enough to gain God's favor — it's one's actions that God values the most.

This leads to another important facet of Islam, the concept of reward and punishment. As stated earlier, both reward and punishment for one's actions can come in this life and/or the next. The standard for the next life is simple: if one's good deeds outweigh the bad deeds, the person will be received in Heaven; whereas if the bad deeds outweigh the good, in Hell. This is why Muslims are encouraged to ask for God's mercy frequently in this life, as they will not be able to do so after death. Additionally, this mercy will benefit an individual in his or her daily life—both materially and spiritually.

Due to this emphasis, mercy and forgiveness are one of the most frequently mentioned attributes of God in the Quran:

> God does not wrong [anyone] by as much as an atom's weight; and if there be a good deed, He will multiply it, and will bestow out of His grace a mighty reward (4:40).

Muslims are enjoined to be optimistic about their destination in the afterlife because negativity about one's final fate shows a lack of faith in God's mercy. At the same time, Islam does not suggest that every action is forgiven. People who commit sins without God's forgiveness will be punished. Consequences could come in this life and/or the next.

CHAPTER 3

ISLAM AND OTHERS

Islam is different from most religions in that it does not believe its followers will be the only ones to obtain Heaven in the afterlife (2:62). Additionally, it does not allow its followers to judge others' fates, as God will be the only judge. Assuming one knows God's final judgment is close to heresy (6:57; 3:128–129; Sahih Bukhari 004:055:549).

The Quran states: "There is no coercion in religion" (2:256). This is considered an important verse in the Quran because it is interpreted to mean that no individual can be forced to believe in Islam or any religion under any circumstance, and that each individual has a *right* to believe what he or she wants.

The spread of Islam through the Middle East in the seventh century has often been described as being "spread by the sword."

In other words, Muslim armies supposedly conquered the world and forced everyone to convert or die. This is simply not factual. After the Muslims of this era defeated the Byzantine and Persian empires, they expanded across Northern Africa and eventually conquered much of modern-day Spain. There was no specific religious mandate for this. Instead the newly energized Arabs were moving into the power vacuum created by the decline of the other great powers in the region. Under the banner of Islam, the people of the Arabian Peninsula struck out with remarkable speed and energy. The new religion created a sense of unity and purpose that the people of the region had never before known. As with any war, the Arab conquest had examples of brutality, but it succeeded in creating a unified polity not seen in the Mediterranean world since the collapse of Rome and made possible the incredible cultural flourishing that was to follow.

The people of these newly conquered lands slowly began embracing Islam as Muslims settled into these areas. Forced conversion was absolutely forbidden, in accordance with the Quran itself. This edict was followed very closely by the Muslims of this era.

The concept of freedom of religion stems from Islam's view on human rights. The Quran states that every human was created from a single pair, Adam and Eve (7:189); therefore, everyone is equal at their core (49:13). Symbolically, this concept of common parentage is a strong argument against the creation and maintenance of barriers across gender, racial, or national lines. Still, "equal" does not mean "identical." While Islam does acknowledge that some individuals may be born with more intelligence, wealth, or abilities, this does not mean that the person is superior in the eyes of God.

The only criteria God uses to judge people are the individual's piousness and righteous actions. Thus, a poor person can hold a much higher place in the eyes of God than a wealthy person. A humble person who gives to charity is valued more highly than a rich person that does not do righteous deeds (49:13). These deeds include prayer, charity, assistance to the sick or needy, defense of the oppressed and other duties indicated by the Quran. This view is supposed to create a sense of equality in the community. The poor, for instance, should not feel inadequate next to the wealthy as it is deeds, that God loves, not wealth. Such a challenge to privilege creates undeniable equality for every human being, and by extension, entitles everyone to the same common rights and freedoms insofar as God is concerned.

THE CONCEPT OF FREEDOM

Islam mandates basic freedoms for Muslims and non-Muslims alike. Because of the prohibition against institutional hierarchies like those found in the Catholic Church, freedom of thought and opinion were traditionally important to Muslims. Not only must one think for oneself, but one must also free the mind from superstition, corruption, oppression, and fear. Moreover, if these phenomena are present in general society, one has a responsibility to oppose them there as well. To the believer, no part of the public sphere should be left unexamined, lest it be allowed to pose a threat to the spiritual integrity of his community or his own salvation.

At its core, Islam not only insists on a degree of freedom of belief, worship, and conscience, but also insists that one exercise these freedoms. The Quran states:

> Let there be no coercion in religion. Truth stands out clear from error. Whoever rejects evil and believes in God has grasped the strongest bond that never breaks. And God knows and hears all things (2:256).

Here, the Quran begins to build the argument that religion is meaningless if induced by force, because faith, will, and commitment can only be attained through the freedom of thought and choice. This is why Islam presents the Truth of God in the form of an opportunity, and leaves the choice for humans to decide their own course. If they were forced to practice their religion it would not stem from belief and would therefore be just a set of meaningless actions. The Quran states:

> The Truth is from your Lord. Let him who will, believe, and let him who will, disbelieve (18:29).

It is important to note here that people who disbelieve are not to be mistreated or coerced but simply left to their choices. Moreover, this prohibition against compulsion would not only include atheists but people of other religions as well.

In summary, The Quran sets out Islam's basic concepts of freedom and argues in favor of individual freedom of conscience and action, provided, of course, that the individual does not violate the rights of another. In addition, one cannot violate the safety and welfare of the community as they are of the utmost importance in Islam. Anyone who wishes to violate the welfare of the community or an individual are abusing their freedom and deserving of lawful punishment. These violations would include acts of theft, violence, murder, oppression, corruption, and slavery.

CHRISTIANITY AND JUDAISM IN ISLAM

Islam addresses Christianity and especially Judaism in very specific terms. The Quran frequently references adherents of both religions as people who followed legitimate messengers of God, Jesus and Abraham, and were also given holy books, the Bible and the Torah respectively. Hence, the Quran refers to them as "People of the Book(3:64)." The Quran also teaches that God has sent messengers to every group of people who exist on earth. Some Muslim scholars assert that Buddhism and some of the traditional religions of Africa, Australia, and the Americas were once God's true religion, but, as with the Christians and the Jews, moved away from the true revelation over time. This reinforces the Quran's assertions that its teachings are not new, and that Muslims have a kinship with many religions. The Quran states:

> And do not argue with the followers of earlier revelation otherwise than in a most kindly manner—unless it be such of them as are bent on evildoing—and say: "We believe in that which has been bestowed upon us, as well as that which has been bestowed upon you: for our God and your God is one and the same, and it is unto Him that We [all] surrender ourselves (29:46)."

It is because of this, Muslims are supposed to treat people of other faiths with kindness and generosity. In a true Islamic society, non-Muslims are given the status of *Dhimmi*, which means "protected people." These non-Muslims do not have to go to war or pay the 2.5 percent charity tax that Muslims must pay. The amount of *Dhimmi* tax varied in different parts of the Islamic world. It is important to note that not a single Islamic society or country exists currently.

Besides mandating fair and just treatment of Christians and Jews by Muslims, the Quran also addresses them in regards to the afterlife. The Quran says:

> VERILY, those who have attained to faith [in this divine writ], as well as those who follow the Jewish faith, and the Christians, and the Sabians—all who believe in God and the Last Day and do righteous deeds—shall have their reward with their Sustainer; and no fear need they have, and neither shall they grieve (2:62).

Thus, Islamic tradition is notable for its inclusiveness. In addition to the religions specifically mentioned, the passage also includes "all who believe," which can be interpreted as referring to other people outside of the religions mentioned. Muslims are taught that the only thing they know with certainty is that if they live as good Muslims, they will be treated well in this life and the next. The fate of others is outside their knowledge and should be left to God alone.

Along these lines, the Quran warns all Muslims that they should not ridicule or mock other people's belief systems, as each human's beliefs are sacred and made on their own accord. Arguing these beliefs viciously will only provoke anger and hatred toward the Muslim abuser and also could, in turn, cause the individual(s) to hate God and his message as well (6:108).

In sum, a sense of equal and just treatment towards others is an important part of Muslim tradition, particularly towards Christians and Jews. As we shall see, this acceptance of inborn equality does not only apply towards other religions, but to gender as well.

CHAPTER 4

WOMEN IN THE TIME OF MUHAMMAD

Islam is often viewed in the West as a misogynistic religion — one that encourages the abuse and degradation of women. Without question, this is the case in some of the countries where Muslims are the majority. However, a close examination of every Islamic text reveals that Islam actually discourages misogyny in all its forms. Unfortunately, some countries in the Middle East and Asia (pre- and post-Islam) have a long cultural history of male domination and female subjugation, and have not yet shaken these prejudices. In other words, the position of women in some Muslim societies is unconnected to the religious system established by Muhammad.

As in any faith, verses of the Quran and certain sayings of Muhammad are routinely taken out of context and used as justification by some authorities. However, a simple examination of these holy texts reveals women are not only given equal rights but distinct privileges as well. The Quran itself teaches that men and women are considered equal in the eyes of God (3:195). It is important to understand the culture from which Islam began in order to see how revolutionary its attitudes toward women were, and still are to this day.

Before Muhammad was even born, pre-Islamic Arabian culture treated women as slaves, who could be traded for money or used for sex. Families would even bury their female babies alive in order to hide the shame of having a girl. At the same time, rich men would often marry dozens of women in order to prove their status in society. Women were granted no human rights and were even forbidden the right to inherit property.

One of Muhammad's earliest and dearest causes was the emancipation of women, and this put him at odds with the rest of Arabian society. It was due to his position on women's rights that many of Islam's earliest converts were, in fact, women. The Quran adamantly forbade the murder of female children and denied men the ability to marry as many wives as they wanted. The Quran stated to the men of the time that they could marry no more than four women and only under strict conditions. This number may still seem unreasonable in modern times, but at the time it was an intrusive limitation. On top of this, the conditions were even more radical if not impossible to attain. Islam only allowed more than one wife if the women were all in agreement and were treated equally in all respects, receiving equal financial support, property, time, and so on—a balance nearly impossible to achieve. For instance, if a man bought a house for one wife, he would have to buy the same exact house for the others. Ultimately, in regards to multiple wives, the Quran states to men that one wife is the best course (4:3).

It is also critical to understand why a woman of the era would even want to be in such a marriage. Women in ancient Arabia, for the most part, could not hold occupations and did not inherit wealth. If a woman was divorced or widowed, it was very difficult to provide for her children or herself. As such, marrying a husband who could provide for her was important, if not vital. Also, women over a certain age who were considered old or were unable to bear children could also benefit from a plural marriage. Muhammad himself defied tradition when he married the first love of his life, Kadeeja, when she was 40 and he was 25. He remained monogamous to her for 24 years, until her death.

Beyond basic human rights, Islam also granted females the right to inherit and divorce, which they had never possessed before in Arabia. In early Islam, women were encouraged to vote, participate, and express their opinions in politics and communal policies[1]. They even fought in wars when needed. The Quran never prescribes the face veil for women, except for Muhammad's wives, who were treated in a special manner due to their intimate knowledge of Muhammad. Nor were women secluded during his life. They were encouraged to be outspoken and to learn. Muhammad would personally teach women and girls in large groups, so their education would be on par with the men's.

Nevertheless, despite Muhammad's example and teaching, it wasn't long after his death that men started reinterpreting the Quran and Muhammad's sayings to match existing prejudices.

---

1. Al-Shura, or democratic consultation, was introduced by Muhammad from the beginning of his time as a prophet, and these councils often involved women.

Borrowing from Persia and Christian Byzantium, and even reverting back to pagan custom, men started secluding women and discriminating against them. Within 120 years after Muhammad's death, men had largely returned the female population of Arabia to the margins of society, despite Islam's clear, original message. It would take the astounding blossoming of Islamic culture during the "Golden Age of Islam," which began two hundred years after Muhammad's death, to return the rights to women gained during his lifetime.

ADDRESSING WOMEN IN ISLAM

The Quran is one of the few holy books to address women specifically and in conjunction with men. Both the Quran and the sayings/practices of Muhammad address many different women's issues, including their rights in marriage, divorce, family, children, inheritance, work, financial situations, and society. Islamic theology contains over 100 laws pertaining to women's rights. Unfortunately, most of these laws are not practiced in most countries where Muslims are the majority today. Cultural indoctrination and tradition have overridden these very basic teachings that come from the Quran and Muhammad's teachings.

The Quran states very clearly that men and women are equal in the eyes of God and in their duty to Him (33:35). This belief is established in the very first tale regarding humankind—the story of Adam and Eve (2:31–37). The well-known Abrahamic tale as told in the Quran differs in two important ways. According to Genesis, it is Eve who tempts Adam into sinning. In the Quran, Adam and Eve were both tempted and sinned at the same time. This is a critical point, since it means that Adam and Eve were equally responsible and equally at fault. Both were filled with remorse, and their repentance was equally accepted. This is the bedrock for Islam's position that women are morally equivalent to men, and that double standards are not acceptable.

As previously stated, the other major difference between Islam and Christianity is that both Adam and Eve were forgiven, thus eliminating the concept of Original Sin. Islam is very clear in its stance that humans are born as good people (6:164). It is the choices some make as they grow that wear on their own souls. Both men and women earn forgiveness or purification through their own good deeds and prayer. Their actions are equal in the sight of God as is his love for them.

It is from the premise of spiritual equality that Islam reaches its views on women, although in some cases, women are actually given preferential treatment over men. For instance, women are not required to pray in congregation, and are exempt from fasting or praying during their menstrual cycle. These exemptions occur because, while Islam acknowledges that men and women are equal, it also acknowledges that they are different. The main difference is that in the Muslim family, the financial responsibilities of a household fall on the man, while the care of children is typically given to women (though men are not exempt from the care of children). The woman is also considered the manager of the household—though this does not necessarily extend to actual housework. Islamic prescriptions expect men to help with housework and help care for the children, as Muhammad did in his time. Also, men are encouraged to provide a housekeeper or nanny if they can afford it.

Women also have the right to all the levels of education men do, as well as the right to engage in any profession or business of their choosing. In fact, Muhammad's first wife, Kadeeja, was a very successful businesswoman. His second wife, Aisha, become one of the most prominent scholars in early Islamic history and one of the most prominent examples of Muslim women who were involved in governmental politics.

WOMEN, MARRIAGE, FINANCES, AND RIGHTS

Marriage is a sacred bond in Islam. Because of its importance, the subject is addressed frequently and in very specific ways. Men in particular are given several injunctions. First and foremost, they are required by the Quran to be kind to women in general. This is reinforced in Muhammad's own sayings. The directives towards one's own wife are given in much more detail.

A husband is charged with the well-being of his wife, something he must see to with good nature and without condescension. The material well-being of a wife consists of housing, clothing, sustenance, and general care. Her residence must provide her with comfort, privacy, and independence. One should note that these things do not have to be extravagant, but neither should they be well below the husband's means.

Men are also expected to respect certain non-material rights. A wife should be consulted in major decisions in an equitable manner while a husband must also respect his wife's feelings, and show her kindness and consideration. If she feels that there is no longer any love or sympathy in the marriage, she has the right to divorce.

Islam also assumes that many of these rights are easily granted but difficult to attain if the woman has no financial resources. Therefore, the Quran offers a very detailed set of financial rules for women at the time of marriage and responsibilities of her husband. Before that time though, it's her father's responsibility to provide for her and her education. She is, of course free to earn her own living as well.

The following concepts and duties are fundamental teachings of Islam concerning marriage and the financial status of women:

1. The Dowry: This term is somewhat confusing, as some cultures dictate that a dowry is the money given by a woman to a man at the time of marriage. In Islam, before she gets married, the *woman* must be given a dowry by the groom. Typically, the man offers a sum of money he can afford or thinks is appropriate. The woman and her family can then accept the dowry or, if the dowry is not to her liking, she can negotiate a different amount or reject his marriage proposal. The dowry is given in order to provide the woman with her own financial base, independent of her husband. This money can be used in case of an emergency, at leisure, for her family, saved for a later date, or in case there is a divorce and she needs the financial support. This last point is one of the biggest reasons why the man has no rights to access to this money once it is given. Ultimately, the woman has control of the marriage process and can never be forced to marry anyone without her absolute consent.

2. It is recommended the woman keep her own last name. This is to show, symbolically, that a woman has not, and will not, lose her own identity after marriage.

3. A woman should have resources (like a private savings) the husband cannot access. This is where the dowry can be placed, as well as any money earned by the woman. What is critical here is that if a woman works, her money is hers and not her husband's. Any money given to the family or spent on her children or household is considered charity in Islam. This is because the man is supposed to provide the shelter, domestic expenditures, sustenance, and education for his wife and children (4:34). She should have access to his money, but he should not have access to hers. In contemporary terms, she could also choose to have a joint account and share her earnings, but her *right* as a Muslim woman is to have control of her own finances. This is so a man cannot control his wife's life by withholding money. These rules also allow her to divorce without worry of complete financial destitution. Similarly, a woman is allowed to own her own property and to dispose of it without consent of her spouse.

4. Due to her financial independence, a woman should make her own will.

5. She has the right to sexual fulfillment. This is also incumbent on the woman for her husband. A woman can even initiate divorce if this is a chronic problem.

Sex with a spouse is considered a blessing from God, and not something to be ashamed of. It is taught that a couple is actually given blessings from God every time they have sex as long as it's within the confines of marriage. As a side note, contraception is expressly allowed in Islam (Bukhari, 62, 135).

6. A woman has a right to pleasant treatment by her spouse. Muhammad said to his followers: "Best amongst you are those that are best to their wives" (Hadith - Al Tirmidhi).

7. A woman has the right to initiate divorce. In addition, alimony and palimony are mandatory. Women get automatic custody of children aged two and under after divorce, unless there is an extreme situation.

8. Mothers are to be respected first and foremost. Muhammad was quoted as saying: "Paradise lies at the feet of the mother" (Hadith - Al Nasa, Ibu Majah & Ahmad).

9. A woman should receive equal pay for equal work (3:195).

According to tradition, women have certain inalienable rights in Islam that sometimes exceed Western norms. There are additional prohibitions against ruining a woman's reputation and Spousal abuse —both emotional and physical.

THE MODERN REALITY

As observed earlier, all the rights for women enumerated by Islam are useless when not respected and enforced. As is often the case in religion and society, men have successfully allowed certain tenets to be distorted in order to gain what they *think* most benefits them.

With the information age in full swing, however, Muslim men and women are gaining increased access to Islamic literature, and are basing their actions and beliefs on actual Islamic tenets and not the interpretations they have inherited through their culture. Today, more Muslims are learning that women's rights will not be won by rejecting their religion, but by observing it. Large Islamic Feminist movements are gaining momentum in places like Egypt and Syria. Women in these countries are leading their own religious congregations and are considered some of the most learned scholars in the region.

One such organization is *Sisters in Islam* in Malaysia, a think tank dedicated to gender equality through Islamic rulings. Moreover, thinkers like Moroccan sociologist Fatima Nernissi, have challenged religious edicts that subjugate women proving that the evidence used was weak and in lieu of stronger, liberating religious texts.

WOMEN, ISLAM, AND CONTROVERSY

Thousands of books, tracts, poems, and commentaries have been written on the subject of Women in Islam. These works, however, contain a variety of opinions. As mentioned previously, within

Islam, there are very liberal and conservative interpretations of a variety of texts and sources that produce, in turn, a variety of opinions. Some of these issues have been debated for centuries and may never find consensus among the faithful. This is deliberate: there are some issues on which Islam does not provide a hard, definitive line. At its best, it is meant to be a religion that allows for different points of view and different levels of commitment.

With this understanding, the following subjects regarding women are ones that have proved to be controversial or, at the very least, misunderstood. The sources of opinion on each topic that follows are referenced by specific Islamic texts, and the majority scholarly opinion provided.

It is also very important to understand that the Quran was revealed over the course of 23 years and addressed the situations that were occurring at that specific time. While the text and its edicts are meant to be timeless, they should also be read with a certain amount of understanding for the historical context in which they were first written down.

MODESTY, VEILS, AND HEADSCARVES

This is an oft-debated topic in the Islamic world, and many books and essays have been written on the subject[2]. First, there is little or no evidence that the face covering, or *niqab*, is mandated or encouraged in Islam. This was a pre-Islamic practice; one that did not become prevalent until the Abbasid period of Islam (over a hundred years after Muhammad's death and the

---

2. For example, "Women in Islam: Hijab" by Ibrahim B. Syed.

start of the Islamic Golden Age). The majority of scholars do not encourage covering the face. However, the headscarf, or *hijab*, is generally accepted as a mark of modesty and piety on the part of Muslim women.

To understand this Islamic practice of modesty, one must first establish the concept behind head covering. The Quran states:

> Tell the believing men to lower their gaze and to be mindful of their chastity: this will be most conducive to their purity—[and,] verily, God is aware of all that they do. And tell the believing women to lower their gaze and to be mindful of their chastity, and not to display their charms [in public] beyond what may [decently] be apparent thereof; hence, let them draw their head-coverings over their bosoms (24:30–31). . .

Here, modesty is being encouraged. The head coverings mentioned in this passage in Arabic (*khumur*) were fashionable scarves that women wore in Muhammad's time. In these verses, the Quran asks women not to display their "charms" beyond what may decently be apparent. Does this include women's hair? Is the head covering here meant to refer to the fashion at the time, or is it a mandate? Because of uncertainty in the precise meaning of the passage, head covering is often a difficult subject to tackle for Muslim communities.

The concept of modesty, however, is not debated. In Islam, women are supposed to be valued and respected for their intellect, opinion, and actions, not for their sexuality. This is one of the largest misconceptions among non-Muslims. Muslim women are supposed to dress modestly, so that they are taken seriously and not exploited sexually by men. Islam takes the view that women are dehumanized when perceived as sexual objects and valued only for their beauty or sexuality. This is the reason Muslims find it ironic that others often view the head covering as a symbol of male oppression.

Though it should also be mentioned that males are not given a pass in respect to their behavior toward women either. As mentioned in the Quran, men are also asked to "lower their gaze" to preserve the modesty of the women (24:30). Islam takes the position that males are typically weaker when it comes to their sexuality [3]. In this respect, men are not supposed to pretend that sexual urges don't exist simply because they're "religious." Instead, a man is supposed to acknowledge his propensity toward sexual thoughts and "lower his gaze" to prevent him from acting inappropriately toward any woman. More importantly, it is incumbent on him to respect and engage women on an intellectual level, rather than succumb to his basest instincts. On top of all of this, he is also expected to dress and act modestly as well.

It is generally assumed in the West that for women, the head covering and veil are symbols of oppression. In some cases, this is true. Women are forced to wear a veil or head covering in a minority of societies—in particular, Saudi Arabia. However, most women wear it voluntarily as a symbol of modesty and Islamic identity. Interestingly, within some countries where Muslims are the majority, the head covering is seen as "backwards." Some women report that it is easier to wear a head covering in the United States or

---

3. There is some scientific research to support this. See Louann Brizendine, *The Female Brain* (New York: Morgan Road Books, 2006); D.M. Buss, and D.P. Schmitt, "Sexual Strategies Theory: An Evolutionary Perspective on Human Mating," *Psychological Review*, 100 (1993), 204–232.

England than in Jordan or Syria. Some scholars say this attitude is due to the 19th century colonization of the Middle East and South Asia by the French and British. Western concepts of modernization and what a modern woman should look like are still prevalent in the Middle East and elsewhere.

The other side of the coin is the Muslim World's view of the West. The Muslim consensus is that the West consistently emphasizes a woman's sexuality and looks in general. They believe this is the cause of the high rate of eating disorders in younger and older women and that a great deal of money is spent trying to make women feel inadequate so they'll spend more on products. Many Islamic scholars view this aspect of Western culture as degrading to women because it appeals to baser instincts and ultimately leads to its own kind of subjugation. They also believe that in some cases, it can lead to a sexual preoccupation for men and women, one that can lead away from scholarly, charitable, familial, and religious pursuits. While these generalizations may be unfair, few in the western world know that this is how many Muslims abroad view their culture and the United States in particular.

POLYGAMY

Having discussed polygamy in the time of Muhammad, it is important to discuss it in the modern context. To reiterate, the basic Quranic mandate states that if a man is to marry more than one wife he must provide for them equally in all respects. Each woman also has to approve of the arrangement. This requirement makes a plural marriage very difficult, if not impossible. Nonetheless, it is useful to understand the allowance of up to four wives. The Quran reads:

And if you have reason to fear that you might not act equitably towards orphans, then marry from among [other] women such as are lawful to you—[even] two, or three, or four: but if you have reason to fear that you might not be able to treat them with equal fairness, then [only] one (4:3). . .

The reference to orphans in the first sentence is an important one. Marriage here is meant to address the needs of children, first and foremost. Most Islamic scholars interpret this passage as meaning that one can help children by marrying their single mothers and providing for them financially. Scholars have also suggested the verse implies that wealthy men, who may already have a family, may have the additional responsibility to help a destitute, single mother by marrying her, if she approves. At the very least, even outside of marriage, Muslims are encouraged to help single mothers because of the burden they and their children carry. Ultimately, the verse states that unless there is a need to help another woman, it is preferable to have only one wife. The Quranic verse 4:139 states that it is very difficult to treat more than one wife equally; therefore, it is a discouraged but allowable practice.

VIRGINS

Men and women are required to refrain from sexual contact until marriage. Virgins, however, have attained a particularly distinct role in Western consciousness in regards to Muslims; namely, the idea that Muslim men who die as martyrs will receive seventy-two virgins in Heaven. This is not mentioned in the Quran, and there is only one very weak Hadith that mentions virgins. It is so weak that it is considered inappropriate to use in scholarship. To determine whether there is even a concept like this in Islam, it is necessary to examine the relevant passages.

First, the Quran states that *everyone* who goes to Heaven will be given "companions pure" who will have beautiful eyes (56:22). "Purity," in this case, has been translated as "virginity," but this is not accurate. Instead, this purity refers to the pureness of soul. The "beautiful eyes" are allegorical and meant to signify "soulful." It is also important to recognize that the companions will be both male and female. The overall concept is that after a life of service to God, one will be served in beauty and be able to enjoy things in leisure. Additionally, people will also be reunited with loved ones in Heaven (84:9).

As for the sayings of Muhammad, there is only one suggesting that a person will receive 72 companions (*hurees*), and it is not considered an authentic tradition. Even so, the word used does not translate directly as virgin, but instead as "pure companion"— either male or female as mentioned above. Whatever these companions are, they are certainly not exclusive to those martyred, or to someone who commits a suicide bombing as is popularly thought in the West. It is important to note, however, that there are extremists who will use these citations to lure people into committing acts of murder. As one can see, passages can easily be misinterpreted or used improperly if they're not studied thoroughly and within context.

INHERITANCE AND WOMEN IN THE QURAN

The Quran asks that men receive a larger share of an inheritance than women (4:11). This was ordained because men are supposed to be given the financial responsibility of every aspect of home life. Nevertheless, a woman's earnings are her own and cannot be touched by her husband. A woman's earnings are supposed to result in a surplus account for the woman alone. Since men are rarely the sole breadwinners anymore, the inheritance rule has been modified in many cases. As a result of work by the Muslim Women's League and others, some institutions now state inheritance can now be distributed equally.

WOMEN AS WITNESSES IN THE QURAN

Two women are required to bear witness to a contract, as opposed to one man (2:282). This is simply because women at the time were routinely left out of any sort of educational system and were not schooled in reading and writing. It wasn't until Islam's call for the equal education of women that women slowly began receiving the same schooling as their male counterparts. During the medieval period, Women's level of education and their knowledge of business were usually less than that of men's, and such a proclamation may have seemed perfectly rational. At the same time, there are many examples from the life of Muhammad himself in which women provided the sole testimony. Cases and anecdotes can be found that have a single woman's testimony trumping that of several men. In fact, some of Muhammad's sayings were relayed by just one woman: his wife Aisha. Again, there are many arguments to be made on this subject, and any interpretation of the Quran is subject to literary analysis and the necessity of context.

FEMALE CIRCUMCISION

The practice of female circumcision is still practiced in some African countries and even as far away as Indonesia. It is practiced by some Muslims, Christians and animists, and the consequences to the victim can range from moderate to severe. There is, however, no Islamic basis for this practice.

There is a very weak, unreliable tradition of disputed authenticity saying that Muhammad allowed a female circumcision to occur but did not endorse it because it was a pre-Islamic practice. Even if this were true, it would be overruled by the Islamic prohibition against harmful acts toward a human being. Ultimately, one can only reach the conclusion that even in the *least* enlightened of the Islamic kingdoms the practice should have been banned based on the numerous injunctions against committing acts of violence against fellow Muslims.

As mentioned earlier, a wife can divorce her husband if he is not satisfying her sexually. Removing the ability to enjoy sex would be at odds with this verifiable rule. Instead, we must consider the origins of the practice. Female circumcision was a practice started 2000 years ago, long before Muhammad was born; it has remained a part of some cultures—despite prohibitions from countless Islamic scholars. Women's groups and Islamic institutions in developing countries continue the struggle of separating this practice from the religion. Advances are being made, with some countries, like Egypt, having outlawed the practice altogether.

WOMEN IN THE MOSQUE

In congregational prayer, women pray in a group behind the men. This gender separation is not considered to be a sexist arrangement. People in Islamic prayer are lined up shoulder to shoulder. Islamic thought states that this would be distracting for both men and women, since they would be lined up right next to each other, touching constantly. Prayer in Islam also requires one to bend over at a certain part of the prayer. It is not considered appropriate for a man to be situated behind a woman when she is bent over.

Regardless of their location inside the mosque, women at the time of Muhammad engaged him in meaningful and substantive dialogue, exactly like the men. This is important because it shows that Muhammad treated women equally and that their location during prayer was not intended as a symbol of their status. It's also significant that a majority of Muslim scholars suggest that groups of women should be allowed to pray *next* to the group of men, as long as they are separated.

CHAPTER 5

JUSTICE

E qual treatment of women is closely related to the broader concept of justice. Justice is one of Islam's central principles. God commands Muslims to be just:

> Behold, God enjoins justice, and the doing of good, and generosity towards [one's] fellow-men; and He forbids all that is shameful and all that runs counter to reason, as well as envy; [and] He exhorts you [repeatedly] so that you might bear [all this] in mind (16:90).

Justice should permeate every aspect of a Muslim's life, whether in business dealings, politics, the treatment of family, or interactions with outsiders. Maintaining representation and justice for the poor is particularly important. Justice is so imperative that it's taught to come before one's own self-interest—even when it's detrimental to the individual. Personal feelings and prejudice should not stand in the way of the pursuit or distribution of justice (5:8; 4:135).

GOOD CHARACTER

Arguably the most important attribute to be stressed in Islam is good character (B.V8, B73, N6), which is required of all followers of Islam. Lying, cheating, backstabbing, arrogance, and even rudeness are forbidden. On the other hand, forgiveness, kindness, and generosity are stressed. One edict states that a Muslim is someone whom others feel safe around, both in word and deed (B. V8, B73, N45). In addition, a Muslim should only speak good things or keep quiet (B. V8, B73, N48). Muhammad was considered the "walking Quran," because his actions and impeccable character embodied its message. He was also very adamant that compassion and generosity should be major attributes for any Muslim:

> None of you [truly] believes until he wishes for his brother what he wishes for himself (An-Nawawi's Forty Hadith, No. 13).

The first two commandments once again underline action as a major part of Islamic faith. A Muslim who does not display good character is simply not practicing the religion properly because such a person is not embracing the proper attributes of a good Muslim. Islam teaches that these attributes will lead one to a more peaceful life, and at the same time help achieve inner peace as well.

TREATMENT OF ANIMALS

A kind and gentle character should permeate a Muslim's life and be displayed not just to human beings, but also toward the earth, plants, and animals. Life is considered a sacred gift from God. Muhammad related a story to his followers:

> A prostitute was forgiven by God because when she passed by a panting dog near a well, she saw that the dog was about to die of thirst. She took off her shoe, and tying it with her head-cover, she drew out some water for it; so God forgave her sins (B 4:54:538).

Islam has some very specific mandates regarding animals. Regardless of whether they are domesticated animals, wild animals, or livestock, they are to be treated with kindness and without cruelty. Animals are to be given ample food, water, and space. They must also be maintained and tended properly. No animal should be killed needlessly, unless it's for food, safety, or practical purposes, such as control of pests. Hunting for sport alone is discouraged.

ANIMALS AND FOOD

While some Muslims are vegetarians, and being a vegetarian is not forbidden, most do eat meat, as Muhammad did in his time. Only pork and carrion are forbidden. There are, however, very specific rules regarding the slaughter of animals. While it's not a pleasant topic, animal slaughter falls within the realm of regulated conduct, so discussion of it is relevant.

First, no animal is allowed to hear or see the suffering of another. In a slaughterhouse, each animal must be separated from the next one in line. The actual act of taking its life should be done as quickly and painlessly as possible. A Muslim is first supposed to thank God for the life He has provided for His followers and acknowledge the animal as a creature of God (6:188–121).

Muslims are encouraged to eat food that is *Halal*, which means "permissible," and is the Muslim version of the Jewish term "kosher." For food to be considered *halal* means that God was thanked before the slaughter, it was done cleanly, and that the animals were treated with kindness in accordance with the rules as stated above.

CHAPTER 6

THE SPIRITUAL AND THE MATERIAL

Islam calls for a balance between the spiritual life and the physical one, but it also recognizes the difficulty of trying to maintain this balance. "Man cannot live by bread alone" is a Biblical expression often misinterpreted as suggesting that the material life is unimportant, though more properly interpreted, it recommends a more balanced approach to life. Similarly, Islam addresses the need to make money and also addresses the physical demands of sleep, recreation and socializing. It even recognizes the real need for companionship and sex. In Islam, sexual intercourse with a spouse is always considered a blessing from God, not something that is dirty or shameful. It also acknowledges that sex outside of marriage is a real temptation, even for the holiest of people. No person is impervious to temptation and pretending to be above it is considered foolhardy.

Islam stresses that action is required for success in spiritual and material pursuits, the Quran states: "One must take action first, and then trust in God" (3:159). A man once asked Muhammad if he could leave his mount to graze and then pray that God let the animal return. Muhammad answered that he had to *tie his mount up first* and then pray that God would keep him safe (Al Tirmidhi) . This teaching stresses the realities of the world in relation to the spiritual. It also is used to show that one cannot just pray for things to happen; one must take action first. Too much spirituality and religion can lead to neglect of one's own life, which will eventually affect one's religious life. Muhammad often tried to ensure his followers did not pray or fast so much that they ignored their worldly obligations.

Moderation is essential in Islam. The Quran reads: "And thus we have willed you to be a community of the middle way" (2:143). This passage is interpreted to mean that moderation is to be applied in every aspect of life: religion, diet, and work. Mainstream Islam takes the view that too much religion can lead to extremism, while being lazy can lead to stagnation. Both Muslim individuals and communities that keep this balance will be successful and cognizant of man's nature and potential. Still, Islam also acknowledges that there will always be people who transgress these moderate limits and in doing so will fall into error.

SCIENCE VERSUS RELIGION

Seeking knowledge in Islam is incumbent on all Muslims (20:114; 96:1–5). Evidence of God and His will is believed to be given through signs. These signs typically manifest themselves in science, nature, and the universe. Humans are asked to study and reflect upon these signs in order to understand God and His will. Muhammad was quoted as saying, "The scholars are heirs of the prophets."[1] Study and research of any subject should lead one to understand God and His will more deeply. In Islam, studying science can be a form of religious scholarship.

For instance, scientific evidence proves that the universe is expanding and will eventually collapse. Muslims are first encouraged to study this phenomenon and then explore why God may have created the universe in this way. Is this scientific fact one that could have spiritual meaning, or reveal the nature or will of God? Different conclusions can be drawn from this evidence, but the point is that Muslims are encouraged to understand scientific phenomena and how they might lead to an understanding of God. The only difference in how a Muslim views science and the universe and how an atheist scientist typically would, is what or who started the "Big Bang." Everything after that moment could have happened as our science has proven it. Unlike the Bible with its long exploration of God's creation of the world, the Quran's picture of the origins of the universe is less detailed. This has allowed Muslims to embrace discovery with less pressure to reject empirical evidence. While some Muslims have historically struggled with Darwinian notions of evolution, research polls show a growing acceptance of those ideas in many parts of the Muslim world.

Another approach to science and Islam is the study of the Quran in a scientific light. Many scholars have dedicated their

---

1. Abu Dawud, Tirmidhi

lives to studying the scientific ideas found within the Quran's verses[2]. For instance, the Quran reads:

> Are, then, they who are bent on denying the truth not aware that the heavens and the earth were [once] one single entity, which We then parted asunder?—and [that] We made out of water every living thing? Will they not, then, [begin to] believe (21:30)?

This, most Muslim scholars say, refers to the aforementioned Big Bang theory, which asserts that the universe was created from a single dense state, which then expanded to create the universe. The Quran also states:

> And it is We who have built the universe with [Our creative] power; and it is We who are steadily expanding it (51:47).

Evolution is not out of bounds for Islam, although the evolution from, say, *Orrorin* to *Homo sapiens* is debated within the faith. Some Muslim scholars suggest that animal and plant evolution are metaphors for humans to understand their ability to evolve and adapt in their lifetime, and that, in fact, they must. This is just one example of how Islam can embrace science and education.

The Islamic search for knowledge led early Muslims to one of the most creative periods in the history of the world—"The

---

2. Muslims have varying degrees of belief about ethereal and mystic subjects. Phenomena like demons and ghosts are often considered metaphors for man's inner fears or reckless inclinations, while others actually believe in the entities themselves.

Golden Age of Islam." For roughly 600 years, starting in the 8th Century, the Islamic Empire ushered in such public institutions as hospitals, libraries, and the first degree-granting universities. While Europe was in the dark ages, cities like Damascus, Cordoba, and Baghdad were thriving centers of civilization. The Muslims created an early form of the scientific method, which led to great strides in the fields of astronomy, medicine, and mathematics. These same scholars subsequently created algebra and developed trigonometry and geometry.

While Islamic civilization was the center of learning, art, and literature during this period, it is also important to note that it was Islam's acceptance of other religions and embrace of free speech and freedom of thought that truly helped propel the accomplishments of the era. Jewish and Christian scholars flocked to the Islamic empire and contributed to the many advancements of the period. The Muslim city of Cordoba, Spain, in particular, was a haven for scholars and artists of all religions to collaborate and flourish, and was considered by contemporaries to be the most beautiful city in the world.

The drive to learn and collaborate was a direct result of the Quran's and Muhammad's teachings. Many modern-day Muslim scholars claim that original Islamic doctrine is exactly what is missing in countries where Muslims are prevalent. Their belief is that a lack of authentic Islamic teachings continues to lead to stagnation of educational and economic development.

CHAPTER 7

MUSLIM COUNTRIES AND GOVERNMENT

There is not a single Islamic government in the entire world; that is, one that was modeled purely after Muhammad's example. The complex history of social dynamics in the Middle East and beyond has left almost all of the 55 countries with a Muslim majority with dictators or repressive regimes — despite the promise of the Arab Spring. The outcome of these regions' history is at odds with basic Islamic teaching. In fact, the closest thing to an ideal structure for an Islamic government is probably the United States, as the American system of government embraces many of those rights and responsibilities put forward in the Quran. This is a controversial assertion in some Islamic circles, as the United States' government does not adhere to the Quran and teachings of Muhammad. It is also a controversial assertion in the U.S. due to rising paranoia regarding the role of Sharia (Islamic Law) and U.S. jurisprudence. While such fears are beyond ridiculous, the truth is there are many basic principles that Islamic law shares with the West: freedom of speech, human rights, public consensus, voting, and the value of social and military services.

Freedom of speech is a core Islamic value as suggested by the Abu Hurayra – Sahih Muslim and Bukhari Hadiths. The Quran states: "[Always] speak with a will to bring out what is just and true..." (33:70). The uproar and threats that arose over Danish cartoons in 2005 are inconsistent with this simple injunction. Threatening or harming anyone because of individual expression is almost absurd considering Muhammad was almost killed many times for expressing himself. In fact, any Muslim would be hardpressed to challenge the right to this type of expression. Nevertheless, the *intent* of an individual's expression can be questioned, particularly if it's purposely misleading or promotes hatred or violence. However, rioting and violence over self-expression should be unacceptable in Islam.

This modern-day violence has sprung from a feeling of powerlessness among some Muslims. These people have no say in their home countries, which are often dictatorships, nor do they have much say in the western countries (i.e. France, Germany, Holland and England) where they flee to in order to escape this tyranny and often find themselves as conspicuous minorities. Muslims still remember a once proud, thriving society that ruled much of the world for a thousand years, and this relegation has led to a pressure-cooker situation in many parts of the world. Frustration and a feeling of impotence have caused many to lash out in desperation, despite what Islam teaches: behaviors antithetical to Muhammad's example.

PUNISHMENT IN A REAL ISLAMIC SOCIETY

An ideal Islamic society would be one governed by democracy and the rule of law. While a more liberal application of law is more desirable among Muslims, transgressions of the law would lead to punishment. Some of the prescribed traditional punishments are controversial. The two harshest punishments explicitly mentioned in the Quran are cutting off a hand for thievery and the penalty of death for adulterers. While these punishments seem barbaric by modern standards, one must understand the conditions that must be met in order to warrant these actions.

The removal of a hand for thievery, for example, is only permissible if several conditions are met. First, of course, there must be a legitimate Muslim government in place. Second, employment and money must be readily available to *everyone* in the society. Only then can one accuse a person of stealing purely for wealth's sake, which is the last condition for punishment. Stealing food to feed one's family is not punishable, as it runs counter to Islam's concept of mercy and is also an indication that the conditions for punishment have not been met. Since it is next to impossible to achieve these conditions, the edict serves more as a serious warning to those considering major theft, as it's a selfish act that hurts both the victim and the society. Still, some countries continue the practice of hand amputation despite vehement refutation of Islam's most accomplished scholars.

Death as punishment for adultery is actually overturned by

the Quran itself, when it is suggested that the couple caught in *flagrante dilicto* should merely be lashed (24:2). However, Muhammad did allow an execution before the verse was revealed, as it was the law at the time. The matter is quickly closed by a careful reading and has been written about extensively. It is also worth noting that the accusation itself requires four witnesses in order to prove the event occurred. Since this is next to impossible, the consensus is that this edict was meant to serve as a severe warning and to emphasize how detestable adultery is according to Islam.

There is also a misconception by some that the penalty for leaving Islam for another religion, or apostasy, is death. This is patently false, as it violates the Quranic assertion that… "there is no coercion in religion" (2:256). Though frowned on, the Quran provides no direct support for the punishment of apostasy either. An individual or government that claims otherwise is in error.

All in all, the conditions required to violate the above laws in a manner demanding punishment could only occur in an almost Utopian Islamic Society where all the poor are cared for, everyone is treated equally and the proper government structure is in place. While these conditions are next to impossible to attain, and have proven illusive in history, there has been quite a lot of thought put into what would constitute the proper structure of an Islamic government.

ISLAMIC GOVERNMENT

There have been many models suggested by scholars for an Islamic democracy, but the lack of a single modern-day, authoritative body in Islam allows for a good deal of disagreement. Muslim scholars from Indonesia to Albania have weighed in on the matter, and the nations of the Middle East hardly represent the final word on the subject.

Almost all scholars agree that the source for an Islamic democracy lies with Muhammad's use of consultative decision-making, or Shura. The Quran also states "And take counsel with them in all matters of public concern; then, when thou hast decided upon a course of action, place thy trust in God. . ." (3:159). When Muhammad established the first Islamic state in Medina in 622 C.E., he drew up a constitution that drew upon revelation but at the same time sought to build consensus among the different tribes and religions that lived in the city. This is significant because Muhammad's constitution attempted to create a community of diverse believers under the aegis of their common monotheism. These constituents included new immigrants to Medina, the inhabitants of Medina, and, significantly, the Jews of Medina who were a minority. The final social contract granted equal rights for all religions and people, including women. It obliged the community to take care of the sick, poor and vulnerable. The constitution itself even insisted on consensual government by the people.

It is interesting to note that all modern-day attempts at forming a supposed Islamic government run counter to the original constitution of Medina. Governments like the one the Taliban in Afghanistan established have been intolerant toward women and other religions. They are also rigid in their interpretation of religious law, with only the governing body's opinion of Islam being considered, not that of the larger community. Other dictatorships and monarchies have tried to reconcile their governments with a version of Islamic principles in an attempt to deflect the attentions of their subject populations, often by encouraging a version of religious fundamentalism that keeps people's attentions focused on religious matters rather than those involving political corruption and oppression. Of course, all have failed to emulate Muhammad's example due to the fact that these governing entities are not compatible with his teachings.

Difference of opinion about forms of government has caused a great deal of unrest in the Muslim world. Unsurprisingly, adherents to original Islamic doctrine disagree with the more extreme groups, who they accuse of misinterpreting Islam. Furthermore, mainstream or moderate Muslims have also started to speak up against the current state of affairs in Muslim countries. This has caused some governments to commit mass killings and, in countries like Egypt, Syria and Libya, to engage in government-sponsored torture and murder. It was the growing gulf between the popular will and stagnant, dictatorial apparatuses that led to the "Arab Spring" — the series of revolutions that began in Tunisia during late 2010 and spread across the Middle East. It is yet to be seen what kind of governments will emerge from these events, but Islam was one of the catalysts for this movement. This fact is often overlooked by the media at large.

It also has to be mentioned that the end to oppression of the governments overthrown during the 'Arab Spring' has given a fresh political energy to several radical subsets of Muslims across the region as well. The jailing, torture and assassinations committed by the old regimes only served to fan the flames of these groups who, armed with a misinterpretation of Islamic texts, have created what some today call "Islamic" extremism.

CHAPTER 8

WAR AND TERROR

It is undeniable that there is a tiny segment of modern-day Muslims who commit terrorist acts. This is actually a new phenomenon that Islam had not seen until the 20th century. The consensus of everyone from Islamic scholars to the U.S. government is that these terrorists are small in number and that their religious interpretations are unsupported. These extremists do, however, have a huge impact on the perception of Islam and its followers. In an age where it only takes one person to create havoc, it is easy to create news. This problem is not exclusive to Islam: people like Anders Breivik, a Christian Terrorist, also engaged in a campaign of terror that was fed by a twisted religious conviction, but terror groups claiming Islamic sanction have come to dominate the public discourse on the subject.

The following section will take chapters in the Quran that are used by these "Muslim" terrorists and attempt to place them in more complete context. Ironically, these are the same chapters that anti-Islamic groups use as proof of Islam's "violent tendencies." All of this despite the fact both groups have twisted the real meaning of these chapters. In His proclamations, Muhammad made no allowances for the types of violence that some associate with Islam today.

While Islam does not encourage senseless violence, it does allow for national and personal self-defense. The Quran, in particular, is very straightforward about the use of force for defending oneself or one's community. The verses that follow were revealed to Muhammad at a time when pagan armies had attacked the newly-formed Muslim communities in Medina and declared war on them. It is critical to establish that Islam never tolerates physical aggression or aggressive wars, only defensive action. Muhammad himself never fought an aggressive war. His earliest efforts aimed towards peaceful coexistence with the inhabitants of surrounding communities, and His followers undertook military operations following the declarations of war by their neighbors. In other words, He only fought in self-defense.

JIHAD

Jihad is not only one of the words most misunderstood by non-Muslims, but also one of the words most abused by radical extremists. The term translated literally means "struggle", or "striving." Its primary meaning is that of an inner struggle, the struggle within oneself: first, to fight the inclination to do wrongful deeds; and second, to establish constancy in achieving righteous actions. These actions can include good treatment of a neighbor, volunteer work, or even political activism. The Quran uses the word "jihad" 33 times in very different ways. Sometimes jihad refers to the struggle for repentance, righteous deeds, and physical migration to a safe homeland.

Muslim scholars often list five types of jihad:

1. Jihad of the soul/heart, known as "the greater jihad," is an inner struggle of good against evil in one's mind and within oneself for self-improvement and coming closer to God.

2. Jihad of the tongue is the struggle to do good and forbid the bad. This includes regular conversation or speech. Muslims are also meant to refrain from gossip and backbiting in everyday life.

3. Jihad of the pen is the struggle of scholarly study. This can include the study of Islam or any other subject, such as science or art that illuminates God's will or helps mankind.

4. Jihad of the hand is the struggle to use economic power to uplift the conditions of the poor and to finance a struggle for justice and liberation.

5. Jihad of the sword, the physical fight against aggression (self-defense) or oppression.

The jihad of the sword is *not* a war against other religions, though the concept is occasionally and mistakenly interpreted as being a call to "holy war". It is certainly not, as some have asserted, directed at Christians and Jews, since they are considered "People of the Book," or fellow heirs of the Abrahamic tradition. The jihad of the sword can only be applied to a just war, when several criteria are met:

1. Any war must be a defensive war. Islam forbids aggressive war and excesses of any kind (2:190). This means that a distinction between combatants and non-combatants must be made and respected. It follows that medical personnel and supplies must be given safe passage. No use of indiscriminate destruction is allowed; Muhammad forbade his soldiers from poisoning the wells of their enemies due to the indiscriminate death that would result.

2. If oppressors attack Muslims to force them to convert from their faith or drive them from their homelands (22:39–40; 4:75), then jihad of the sword is justified.

3. If a war is taking place, prisoners of war must be treated with respect and dignity. Adequate sustenance must be provided as well (76:9–11).

4. If peace is offered, it must be accepted (8:61–62).

In addition to these criteria, Muhammad ordered that once engaged in jihad of the sword, livestock, crops, places of worship, clergy, and all civilians must be protected.

These restrictions were deliberately put in place to keep Muslims from being aggressors and indiscriminate combatants. Muhammad took great effort to emphasize that peace, dialogue, and scholarship were far preferable to war and fighting whenever possible. Again, one is reminded of Muhammad's famous statements: "The scholars are inheritors of the prophets."

TERRORISM

The modern-day concept of terrorism does not find justification in Islam. Muslims did not kill indiscriminately in war at the time of Muhammad. According to the Quran, every person was created to worship God (51:56). Therefore, killing any person obstructs their true purpose and the killer should be made accountable for it.

There have, however, been rare instances in the 20th century when people calling themselves Muslims killed indiscriminately, despite Islam's tenets. This concept of killing civilians indiscriminately was unheard of in Islam until the 20th century.

One can see by the previous edicts, anyone genuinely committed to Islamic teaching could not condone terrorism. Nevertheless, it is not difficult for people of any religion to twist phrases to suit their needs. Most terrorists, like the late Osama Bin Laden, try to justify their actions by claiming that the violence they perpetrate is defensive because America, or the West at large, is at war with the so-called Islamic World. The problem is that any group of Muslims can claim the war they engage in or the violence they commit is jihad, despite the refutation of an overwhelming majority of lay-Muslims and Muslim scholars. Even if this majority endorsed a "just war," the indiscriminate killing of civilian men, women, and children would be forbidden, as dictated in Islam. It should go without saying that suicide, and therefore suicide bombing, is also strictly forbidden (B 8:78:647). The Quran states very plainly:

Don't take a life which Allah has made sacred except by way of justice and law: this He has enjoined upon you so that you might use your reason (6:151).

It would be proper to say that most religions have had adherents who have acted in their own interests and improperly used religion as an excuse for their atrocities. Along these lines, it is unfair to judge any religion by its followers alone. Critique of a religion should examine fundamental tenets and texts. Islam has not been immune to abuse by extremists or people who willingly misinterpret the Quran for their own interests. The following section lists almost every verse in the Quran that is commonly misinterpreted by anti-Muslim groups to prove that Islam encourages terrorism. Interestingly, extremist Muslims use some of the same verses to prove their tactics are viable. Careful study of each verse in context proves both groups wrong.

Although the following section may be dense, examining all the controversial verses will result in a more plausible study of terrorism in Islam. Once again, it is important to establish that Islam does not encourage or condone aggression, a factor that must be considered when studying any verse that addresses war and violence. The Quran clearly states:

And fight in God's cause against those who wage war against you, but do not commit aggression—for, verily, God does not love aggressors (2:190).

The next verse is one used by almost every anti-Islamic group. Taken out of context, it may look unreasonable, but when read with its preceding verses, it's clearly taking a stance against aggressors and towards peace:

> And slay them wherever you may come upon them, and drive them away from wherever they drove you away—for oppression is even worse than killing. And fight not against them near the Inviolable House of Worship (Mecca) unless they fight against you there first; but if they fight against you, slay them: such shall be the recompense of those who deny the truth (2:191). But if they desist—behold, God is much-forgiving, a dispenser of grace (2:192).

If one were to read the first verse, 2:191, out of context, it would look unreasonably violent and tyrannical. But in context, "slaying" clearly refers to people who have aggressively attacked the Muslims or have waged war against them. Ultimately, these verses prove that Islam only allows fighting in self-defense when an enemy is oppressing the people. What extremist Muslims will say is that America has been oppressing the entire world, and that this injunction should be applied to the U.S. This is a big, uninformed leap in logic, but one that can be exploited with some people.

Of course, the last part of the passage is rarely mentioned by either extremists or anti-Islamic groups. It requires that if the enemy desists from killing and oppression, the Muslims must stop as well.

The Quran is also very clear when it comes to people who believe differently but do not wage war against Muslims:

As for such [of the unbelievers] that do not fight against you on account of [your] faith, and neither drive you forth from your homelands, God does not forbid you to show them kindness and to behave towards them with full equity: for, verily, God loves those who act equitably (60:8).

The assertion that Islam does not tolerate other religions and seeks to conquer the entire world is simply incorrect. There is no textual evidence for either claim. In fact, as pointed out before, the Quran clearly states, "There is no coercion in religion" (2:256). Muslim scholars unanimously understand this verse as meaning that no one can force another human being to follow any religion. It is incumbent on Muslims not to force conversion or allow others to do so.

The Quran also addresses what one should do if someone breaks a peace treaty with Muslims:

As for those with whom thou hast made a covenant, and who thereupon break their covenant on every occasion, not being conscious of God; if thou find them at war [with you], make of them a fearsome example for those who follow them, so that they might take it to heart; or, if thou hast reason to fear treachery from people [with whom thou hast made a covenant], cast it back at them in an equitable manner: for, verily, God does not love the treacherous! And let them not think—those who are bent on denying the truth—that they shall escape [God]: behold, they can never frustrate [His purpose] (8:56–59).

This verse refers only to people who have broken a peace treaty with Muslims, double-crossed them, or engaged them in war. The passage continues:

> Hence, make ready against them whatever force and war mounts you are able to muster, so that you might deter thereby the enemies of God, who are your enemies as well, and others besides them of whom you may be unaware, [but] of whom God is aware; and whatever you may expend in God's cause shall be repaid to you in full, and you shall not be wronged (8:60).

Taken by itself, this would seem to be an ominous warning for non-Muslims. However, when read with the previous section, it is clear that this verse refers to people who have broken a treaty and started a war. To fully understand the teaching, one must read the next verse:

> But if they incline to peace, incline thou to it as well, and place thy trust in God: verily, He alone is all-hearing, all-knowing (8:61)!

Again, this verse shows that even during a war, if the enemy of a Muslim society wants peace, the Muslims must comply with that wish. In other words, the default position of any Muslim society or community should be one of peace and that Muslim nations should always be on the side of encouraging good relations between neighbors regardless of creed or confession.

The following verse is challenging because if one does not

read the preceding verses or understand that the verse was revealed at a time of war, it seems to encourage violence against
almost anyone:

> Now when you meet [in war] those who are bent on
> denying the truth, smite their necks until you overcome
> them fully, and then tighten their bonds; but thereafter
> [set them free,] either by an act of grace or against ran-
> som, so that the burden of war may be lifted: thus [shall it
> be]. And [know that] had God so willed, He could indeed
> punish them [Himself]; but [He wills you to struggle] so
> as to test you [all] by means of one another (47:4) . . .

First, one must note that the statements made here refer to
the conduct of war alone. As mentioned previously, Muslims can
only fight a defensive war. In this verse, the expression "smite
their necks" might be interpreted to mean "slay" or "fight." This
should not be read literally, and is not an exhortation to literally
behead one's perceived enemies. Instead, all acts of war and conflict should be undertaken with the same restraint advocated by
the previously mentioned verses. The term "tighten their bonds"
refers to prisoners of war. The verse permits the capture of prisoners of war as opposed to the complete, senseless slaughter of all
combatants or civilians.

The following verse forbids the murder of innocents:

> Because of this did We ordain unto the children of
> Israel that if anyone slays a human being—unless it be

[in punishment] for murder or for spreading corruption on earth—it shall be as though he had slain all mankind; whereas, if anyone saves a life, it shall be as though he had saved the lives of all mankind. And, indeed, there came unto them Our apostles with all evidence of the truth: yet, behold, notwithstanding all this, many of them [1] go on committing all manner of excesses on earth (5:32),

The continuation of the passage is often misunderstood and mistranslated:

It is but a just recompense for those who make war on God and His apostle, and endeavor to spread corruption on earth, that they are being slain in great numbers, or crucified in great numbers, or have, in result of their perverseness, their hands and feet cut off in great numbers, or are being [entirely] banished from [the face of] the earth: such is their ignominy in this world. But in the life to come [yet more] awesome suffering awaits them (5:33).

Here, with the proper translation, it is easy to see that the Quran is discussing what has happened to those who have waged an aggressive war on God's people. Anti-Muslim groups have interpreted this as a legal command to Muslims, but this charge is absolutely false. It's also important to note that in classical Arabic, the term "their hands and feet cut off" is meant to suggest that their power has been taken from them.

---

1. "Them" here refers to followers of the Bible, both Jews & Christians.

Here is another passage that can be isolated to look ominous:

> How, then, could you be of two minds about the hypocrites, seeing that God [Himself] has disowned them because of their guilt? Do you, perchance, seek to guide those whom God has let go astray—when for him whom God lets go astray thou canst never find any way (4:88)?

In context, "hypocrites" refers to some people who had migrated with Muhammad from his home city of Mecca to his new home in Medina. They were people who said they were close to him but really supported the pagans who meant him harm. The passage continues:

> … Do not, therefore, take them for your allies until they forsake the domain of evil for the sake of God; and if they revert to [open] enmity, seize them and slay them wherever you may find them. And do not take any of them for your ally or giver of succor (4:89),

> unless it be such [of them] as have ties with people to whom you yourselves are bound by a covenant. . . Thus, if they let you be, and do not make war on you, and offer you peace, God does not allow you to harm them (4:90).

> . . . Hence, if they do not let you be, and do not offer you peace, and do not stay their hands, seize them and slay them whenever you come upon them: for it is against these that We have clearly empowered you [to make war] (4:91).

The permission to take life only refers to people who have actively declared war or "reverted to open enmity" against Muslims. This does not apply to anyone who had a peace treaty, as it was forbidden to break a peace. It was, however, critical for the Muslims to defend themselves from people who were eager to decimate the fledgling community. Nevertheless, it must be emphasized that the Quran consistently ordains that enemies who call for peace must not be harmed.

The following verse has also been quoted many times as unreasonably brutal, and it does appear to be so, if read out of context:

> Lo! Thy Sustainer inspired the angels [to convey this, His message, to the believers]: "I am with you!" [And He commanded the angels:] "And, give firmness unto those who have attained to faith [with these words from Me]: `I shall cast terror into the hearts of those who are bent on denying the truth; strike, then, their necks, [O believers,] and strike off every one of their finger-tips!' (8:12)"

This verse refers to an occasion in which Muhammad's followers were going to war against a vastly superior army. The revelation then came to them that God had told the angels to strengthen the hearts of the believers. This is meant in a strictly spiritual sense. There is no evidence in the Quran or in any other record that angels actually fought in a battle. Angels convey this message because God does not talk to any human directly.

The word "terror" in this verse may be reason for pause, but it is critical to understand that this passage does not refer to terrorism in the modern sense of the word. Here, God is telling the Muslims that *He* would fill their enemies' hearts with fear, so they could "strike, then, their necks (O believers) and strike off every one of their finger-tips." This, of course, meant "to destroy the army." This phrase in Arabic was a common metaphor used during the period. There is no historical evidence that anyone was actually beheaded or had his fingers cut off. In fact, mutilation of combatants and the dead was forbidden. The expression simply gave permission to the Muslims at the time to fight their enemy without fear, knowing they were on the side of the right.

After the early Muslims established their nation, verses were revealed to address how the state would be run. At the time, Islam was struggling for survival in a veritable sea of pagans who threatened to destroy the community of believers.

> [And] fight against those who—despite having been vouchsafed revelation [aforetime]—do not [truly] believe either in God or the Last Day, and do not consider forbidden that which God and His Apostle have forbidden, and do not follow the religion of truth [which God has enjoined upon them] till they [agree to] pay the exemption tax with a willing hand, after having been humbled [in war] (9:29).

Here, the Quran tells the Muslims that non-Muslims (*al-dhimmi,* or "protected people") in an Islamic State have to pay the *Jezia* tax. At first glance, this would seem unfair, until one understands exactly how the Islamic State is to be run. In an Islamic State, able-bodied Muslims are required to take up arms when a just and defensive war has ensued. Since this is considered a religious obligation, non-Muslims do not have to go to war at all.

The *Jezia* tax was simply a poll tax that gave non-Muslims the right to be protected by the government. In exchange, non-Muslims were guaranteed all their civil rights and religious freedoms. In some cases, Muslims had to pay higher taxes and serve in the military as well. The amount of tax was calculated based on the time and place. Some non-Muslims were notably exempt from the *Jezia* tax altogether:

1. All women
2. Men who had not reached maturity
3. Elderly men
4. Sick or crippled men
5. Priests and monks
6. Any non-Muslim who volunteered for the army

It is clear that Islam saw non-Muslims as having the same rights as Muslims in an Islamic society, if not more. Yet, the following verse may make it seem otherwise:

> O you who have attained to faith! Do not take the Jews and the Christians for your allies: they are but allies of one another and whoever of you allies himself with them becomes, verily, one of them; behold, God does not guide such evildoers (5:51).

Again, this passage refers to the various Christian and Jewish tribes who were fighting against the Muslims at that very specific time in Muhammad's life. It was certainly not a blanket ruling against being friends with Jews and Christians, as evidenced in the following verses:

As for such [of the unbelievers] as do not fight against you on account of [your] faith, and neither drive you forth from your homelands, God does not forbid you to show them kindness and to behave towards them with full equity: for, verily, God loves those who act equitably. God only forbids you to turn in friendship towards such as fight against you because of [your] faith, and drive you forth from your homelands, or aid [others] in driving you forth: and as for those [from among you] who turn towards them in friendship; it is they, they who are truly wrongdoers (60:8–9)!

CONCLUSION

It is easy to see how certain verses in the Quran can look unreasonable, violent, or ominous. They were written down at a time in Islam's past that was rife with conflict. Consequently, it's important that anyone reading the Quran take into account the historical context in which it was revealed. Much more detailed books and essays can be found at the end of this book on the subject of war and terrorism, but the best way to study the subject is by reading the Quran itself- preferably in Arabic. The Arabic used in the Quran is very rich and very different from today's colloquial dialects. A one-word adjective in classical Arabic would require an entire sentence in other languages. If one cannot read the Quran in Arabic, it is best done with a good translation and annotation. The Muhammad Asad translation and annotation, used for this book, is considered by many to be the best in available in English.

CHAPTER 9

THE FIVE PILLARS OF ISLAM

It is said that Islam is like a building that stands on five foundations, or pillars. These pillars are the five principle practices of Islam, the actions and beliefs that make a Muslim a Muslim.

1. Witnessing *(Shahaada)*: The term *Shahaada* is actually a complete sentence in Arabic, which in many ways describes Islam as a whole. This sentence, when declared with belief, is what makes a person a Muslim. It is considered so important that its declaration is the only requirement for someone to convert to Islam. When *"shahaada"* is stated aloud and with conviction, Muhammad promised that the new Muslim is forgiven for all his/her previous sins when they become Muslim. At that moment, it is believed that this person is spiritually new as the day they were born. It should be noted that Muslims do not really believe that one converts to Islam, but rather one simply reverts back to humanity's natural inclination toward God and His laws. The phrase is simply this: "There is no god but God, and Muhammad is His messenger."

This statement, at first, does not seem terribly complex, but the person who says it with belief is expected to understand its implications. The first half of the declaration, "There is no god but God," proclaims that nothing else has real power and control in the universe, that the laws of chemistry, physics, and biology are God's laws alone. This belief includes the acknowledgement that God has created laws for humans as well, and that these laws should be followed. Nothing or no one else is to be worshipped.

The second half of the declaration, "Muhammad is His messenger," acknowledges Muhammad as the final legitimate messenger of God. Because of this, Muhammad is also called "The Seal of the Prophets" as Islam teaches that he was the last prophet that will be sent to humankind. Equally important is the acknowledgement that it's through Muhammad's example that people know the specifics of practicing Islam. In fact, it was Muhammad who illustrated how the following four pillars were to be practiced.

2. Prayers *(Salat)*: Prayer in Islam is considered one of the most important pillars, as adult Muslims are supposed to pray five times a day: before sunrise, a little past noon, late afternoon, at sunset and at night. The frequency is meant to show a consistent awareness of God as well as constant dedication.

Muslim prayer contains an essential spiritual component, but it is also combined with very specific physical actions. First, one is to wash before prayer. This is meant to have two benefits: it is supposed to represent a spiritual cleansing and renewal, as well as being a practical hygienic cleansing with its own obvious benefits (the removal of dirt, smell, and germs).

The prayer itself has the same duality. In the spiritual sense, the prayer should strive to attain several goals. It establishes a daily discipline and consistent connection to God. The fact that the prayer is performed throughout the day offers a small break from worldly realities by providing a chance to reset priorities and gain perspective. Islam also teaches that it's a way in which to praise God, seek His forgiveness, and ask for His guidance. Lastly, like prayers in other faiths, it's also a chance to make requests: whether these are good health, peace, or more material concerns.

The physical actions of the prayer itself are also a form of light, daily exercise. The standing, bowing, and prostration during prayer utilize every muscle in the body[1]. The actions are slow and deliberate; relaxing, stretching, and calming the body. It is also meant to be a physical display of human humbleness before God.

In addition to the specific movements accompanying prayer, every Muslim around the world prays in the direction of the city of Mecca (the place where Abraham was said to have built a mosque for God). Praying at the same times and in the same direction provides a sense of unity for Muslims, no matter their ethnicity or location. Logistically, at a given time or place, Muslims are always facing in the same direction and praying to God somewhere in the world at the same moment. Because of this, the ritual creates a powerful sense of belonging.

---

1. Ibrahim B. Syed, "The Medical Benefits of Taraweeh Prayer," www.islamfortoday. com/syed03.htm.

Muslims are also allowed to pray anywhere on earth, and no particular holy place (or mosque) is required. Each individual prayer typically takes about five to ten minutes.

3. Charity *(Zakaat)*: The word *Zakaat* in Arabic actually goes beyond the common concept of charity. It is an essential part of the entire economic system of Islam. On its most basic level, *Zakaat* is 2.5 percent of one's surplus wealth, given once a year. To make the distinction, it is not two percent of one's yearly income, only the extra income or savings after expenses. People who are unable to afford it are not required to give.

Traditionally, *zakaat* is distributed to the following groups: one's family, the poor, orphans, widows, and the disabled. As time has gone on, its role has expanded to supporting community services such as education, libraries, and health care in Muslim countries.

On a more philosophical level, *Zakaat* is seen as the purification of wealth. Since wealth is given by God's providence, it should partly be used for the benefit of humanity. While *Zakaat* is the minimum someone with surplus wealth can give, additional giving is encouraged (2:195). Giving should be done humbly, without showing off in lavish displays (2:264–265).

As mentioned earlier, making money and becoming wealthy is perfectly acceptable in Islamic teaching. Buying goods and enjoying one's wealth is not a sin in and of itself. Only extravagance and disregard for charitable giving are forbidden. It is also considered a sin to indulge in economic exploitation. Islam is very conscious of the difficulties that debt can bring to working people. While it is mandatory to repay loans, charging someone interest is forbidden. This is because it heaps excess debt on top of someone who was needy in the first place.

This view of interest even applies in a business setting. In the Islamic system of loans, a profit can be made only if the lender is exposed to the same risks as the borrower. If the business prospers, the lender gets his or her original investment back, as well as a share of the company's profits. At the same time, if the business fails, the lender has to bear a proportionate share of the losses of the amount loaned.

Finally, the poor people at the time of Muhammad were concerned that God would favor wealthy people because of the amount they gave in charity. Muhammad assured them there were all kinds of charity not requiring wealth or money. He was quoted as saying:

> Indeed the gates to goodness are many: glorifying God, praising Him, magnifying Him, saying "There is no god but God," enjoining the good and forbidding the wrong, removing (any source of) harm from the road, making the deaf hear (and understand), guiding the blind, showing the seeker his need, striving as far as your two legs could carry you and with deep concern to give succor to him who asks, carrying with the strength of your arms (the burdens of) the weak. All these are (acts of) charity.

He added:

> And your smiling in the face of your brother is charity, your removing of stones, thorns, and bones from people's paths is charity, and your guiding a man gone astray in the world is charity for you.[2]

---

2. From the Fiqh us Sunnah collection of Hadith, vol. 3, #98

Not everyone has the ability to donate money. The idea that charity extends beyond money and wealth is a critical one because it provides all people the dignity of contributing.

4. Fasting *(Sawm)*: Fasting is reserved mainly for the month of Ramadan in the Islamic calendar, which is a lunar calendar (2:183–187). Fasting is also encouraged at any time in the year, as long as it is not done to excess.

Fasting is relatively simple in Islam. One cannot eat, drink, or have sexual relations during daylight time (sunrise to sunset). This is not to say that Islam sees these things as evil. In fact, it acknowledges them as the most fundamental of human needs, and because they are fundamental needs, refraining from them is considered a great act of self-discipline and sacrifice. The absence of food and drink is also supposed to remind Muslims of what truly needy people feel every day, and what a gift from God food and water really are.

While fasting is incumbent upon every Muslim, it is not supposed to be torturous. One cannot extend the fast beyond sunset. It is also forbidden to fast if one is sick, traveling, too young or too old, mentally incapacitated, or if it endangers one's life. Women are not supposed to fast during their menstrual cycle, and in some cases, during pregnancy (2:222), and while they are breast-feeding.

During the month of Ramadan, Muslims are encouraged to be particularly aware of God, and to practice their faith with renewed earnestness. Ramadan is usually a community event where everyone fasts at the same time and then eats at the same time. Participants are encouraged to start eating with a group in order to share the thankful experience of eating and drinking after a day of fasting. It is also a time when Muslims are supposed to reflect on how they have been living throughout the year. Overall, Ramadan is intended as a time of physical, mental, and spiritual renewal.

5. Pilgrimage (Hajj): Every Muslim in good health and with the financial means must perform a pilgrimage to the holy city of Mecca at least once in their lifetime. There, a series of rituals reminds the believer of events associated not only with Muhammad, but Abraham, who was said to be the original builder of the mosque in Mecca and founding figure in both Judaism and Christianity.

The *Hajj* is also supposed to be an occasion when Muslims from all over the world can see, relate, and communicate with one another. Each pilgrim wears simple white clothing in order to dismiss any display of wealth or class. The simple garb symbolizes the fact that all individuals are equal in the eyes of God, no matter what they own or where they come from.

A FINAL NOTE ON THE PILLARS

The five pillars are tied to one of the original concepts of Islam, the idea that following God's laws will bring true inner peace to an individual. Creating this sense of peace benefits the believer physically, mentally, and spiritually. Muslims believe that through these five pillars, they become closer to God.

WHAT IS FORBIDDEN

While some of the things Islam considers forbidden have been mentioned throughout this book, some items have not fallen neatly into any of the chapters. There are four things that are prominently forbidden: alcohol, pork, adultery, and murder. Most Muslim scholars state that what is forbidden in Islam is forbidden for practical reasons. For instance, drinking alcohol is prohibited because it impairs decision-making, affects reason, and makes it difficult to think about God with clarity. The more obvious reasons are the damage it does to oneself and the increased chance of hurting others. Other things that are prohibited are:

- Muslims are prohibited from eating pork (not unlike the Jewish law), as the pig is an animal whose meat is considered to be unclean and unhealthy. Muslim scientists point out the negative effects this meat has on the body, such as the effect on cholesterol compared to the meat of other animals, and the ability of the pig to transmit epidemic disease.

- Gambling is forbidden for several reasons. Muslims are supposed to earn their money through their own labor. In addition, gambling has an addictive quality with obvious consequences that include losing time and money, often to devastating effect.

- Murder is forbidden. Though killing in self-defense or as a result of a court judgment (capital punishment) is not considered murder. The negative effects of murder are considered numerous and long-lasting, but in addition it is a direct affront to God. If God created man to worship him, an individual who murders is taking away another's ability or potential to worship God. This is why the Quran states that "if anyone slays a human being-unless it be [in punishment] for murder or for spreading corruption on earth-it shall be as though he had slain all mankind; whereas, if anyone saves a life, it shall be as though he had saved the lives of all mankind. (5:32)"

- Adultery is forbidden due to the effect it has on the person's mate and family, as well as the possibility of venereal disease and unwanted pregnancy.

- Idolatry or ascribing partners to God (*Shirk*) is considered the biggest sin in Islam. This means believing God has equal partners, or that anyone or anything has power equal to him. Implicit in this is belief in God himself. There is also a concept of minor *Shirk* which states that one should not pray to other humans, like religious or political leaders, or covet things, like money, as they become minor gods of sorts. One is only supposed to put all of their trust, love, and devotion to the One True God.

CHAPTER 10

MUHAMMAD'S LIFE

The Quran was revealed over the course of twenty-three years, and addressed the issues and situations occurring during Muhammad's lifetime. Nevertheless, these issues and edicts are considered timeless, but at the same time need to be read with this historical context in mind. Understanding Muhammad's life and time period is critical to understanding the Quran and Islam in general. It should be the basis of any attempt to understand the religion. A complete summary of Muhammad's life and experiences lay far beyond the scope of this short overview, of course: His personal life, his treatment of orphans, women, and fellow men have been recorded in very fine detail elsewhere and need not be repeated here. Still, one can get a sense of Muhammad's character and accomplishments by studying the decisions he made at the most important points of his life.

Muhammad ibn Abdallah was born in the year 570 A.D. in the city of Mecca in what is now known as Saudi Arabia. Mecca, at the time, was the center of trade and religion in the Arabian Peninsula. Only two generations earlier, Muhammad's tribe, the Quraish, had been Bedouins who faced a very tough, nomadic survival in the desert. The Quraish and all the other tribes of Arabia lived by a code of conduct called *Muruwah. Muruwah* put the well-being of the tribe first and foremost and required all of the tribe's people to dedicate themselves to it without question. The head of the tribe was to be obeyed at all times. The strong protected the weak. The *Muruwah* code was also a violent and Machiavellian one. If someone killed a member of a tribe, the victim's tribe *had* to retaliate and kill a member of the murderer's tribe. If it did not, the tribe would be seen as weak, and all the other tribes would look at them unfavorably or could even kill them with impunity. This caused widespread outbreaks of tribal warfare and mayhem throughout the entire region.

When the Quraish finally settled in the city of Mecca, they became merchants and traders. Their change of lifestyle essentially made them rich, as Mecca was a major center for all trade in Arabia. Affluence changed the people of the Quraish and their adherence to the *muruwah* code. Money was becoming more important than the old tribal customs. Commerce was bringing new people and new religious practices to Mecca throughout the year. As a result, it became the biggest center for idol worship in the peninsula. People could leave their idols in the center of the city and come back to worship them at any given time.

All of this brought wealth and prestige to the Quraish who were able to obtain new luxuries beyond their dreams. The wealth, however, was concentrated around only a few families while other families were left to struggle for survival. Muhammad's family, the Hashim, was one of the families left to fend for itself.

Muhammad's father died before Muhammad's birth, and his mother died when he was six years old. Muhammad was left in the care of his uncle, Abu Talib, who was the chief of his tribe. Because of this, Muhammad grew up learning the business of commerce. While he could not read, he still learned to conduct business with skill. He was extremely well-liked in Mecca, and his reputation for friendliness and honesty was widespread.

When he turned twenty-five, a forty-year-old widow named Kadeeja hired Muhammad to manage a caravan to Syria. Kadeeja was one of the few women in Mecca who had wealth and status. Most women had neither and were treated little better than chattel.

Muhammad carried out his mission for Kadeeja swiftly and honestly. She was impressed. After making some inquiries around Mecca and learning of his irrefutable character, Kadeeja decided to propose to Muhammad — something almost unheard of at the time. She had been looking for someone who was kind and loving, and did not care about her wealth. Muhammad fit this description perfectly, and they both consented to marriage without hesitation. Muhammad never spoke more highly of a woman throughout his life, and remained by her side for twenty-four years until her death at the age of sixty-four.

It was around this time that Muhammad grew increasingly concerned with the behavior of his fellow Meccans. They were discarding all the good parts of *muruwah*, like loyalty and honor, while maintaining the negative parts, like arrogance, entitlement, and combativeness. He was becoming increasingly disillusioned by the Quraish and increasingly concerned about the role of idol worship in Meccan society. He didn't understand how someone could pray to an inanimate object that could neither help nor harm them. There did exist among the Arabian tribes an abstract belief in al-Lah (translated: The God), the all-powerful God who created the Universe, but the Quraish felt he was too far away, too distant. If there was a great calamity or emergency in their lives, they would pray to al-Lah, but for the most part, they found an all-powerful God they couldn't see or touch unappealing. Money and honor were much more important at the time. These things were not only worshipped in the abstract, but there were physical idols that one could appeal to for them. All these sentiments concerned Muhammad, and compelled him to embark on a spiritual search that would satisfy the restlessness in his heart. He soon began taking walks outside the city to a distant mountaintop, where he would ponder and meditate. It was here he experienced something that would change his life forever.

One night, Muhammad, at age forty, was meditating in his remote place on the mountain. Suddenly, he felt a sense of anxiety and constricted breath. A voice then commanded him to "Read!" Confused, Muhammad refused, as he could not read. He then repeated what he would later tell were the words of God given to him by the Angel Gabriel (In Islam, Gabriel is sometimes referred to as the Holy Spirit of Revelation). The Quran states the command was:

Read! In the name of thy Sustainer, who has created man out of a germ-cell [the fertilized female egg]. Read—

for thy Sustainer is the most Bountiful one who has taught [man] the use of the pen, taught man what he did not know (96:1–5).

This verse stressed that it is God that was all-powerful and He would be the one to teach them things they did not know before. It could be further suggested that this first teaching indicated that reason needed to be the new guide for action and understanding; and that knowledge and scholarship would be critical for the coming times. This revelation and many subsequent ones were disclosed to Muhammad over the course of twenty-three years, and would later be compiled to become the Islamic holy book, the Quran.

After this first revelation, Muhammad went to his wife Kadeeja and told her that he feared he was either possessed or going insane. She replied: "You are kind and considerate to your kin. You help the poor and forlorn and bear their burdens. You are striving to restore the high moral qualities that your people have lost. You honor the guest and go to the assistance of those in distress. This cannot be, my dear."[1]

Muhammad slowly accepted the revelations, and started compiling them by memory. He then started telling the people of Mecca about the religion of al-Lah, the same basic religion God had handed down since the beginning of time. He railed against the paganism and polytheism of his neighbors, and called for a spiritual renewal. This did not go over well with the Meccans.

First, Muhammad was from a lowly clan within the larger

1. Ibn Ishaq and Sirat Rasul Allah, *The Life of Muhammad*, trans. A. Guillaume. New York: Oxford University Press, 2002.

tribal hierarchy of the Quraish. They could not believe God would ever appoint such a lowly person as a messenger. Besides, they had all heard the stories of Jesus and Moses who had performed great miracles, while Muhammad performed none. Also, the early messages of the Quran demanded that an equitable society be formed, where the poor and vulnerable were treated with respect and dignity. Charity to these people and prayer to the One God were to be the law.

The other Quraish did not like this message or being told what to do. They would also watch, horrified, as Muhammad would put his forehead on the ground in prayer to show his humbleness to God. This was considered an incredibly demeaning gesture to them. Still, despite all the aversion, Muhammad attracted a small number of believers. They were drawn to the message that everyone was equal and that intelligence and reason were to be used in understanding the revelations, not ancient codes of conduct. They responded to the idea that the signs of God were all around them if they took the time to inspect and analyze.

Women, youth, and the poor comprised many of the early converts to Islam. The richer people, who were satisfied with their lives and status, did not find a need for it—or for religion in general. Money and tradition were enough for them to be content. Muhammad would occasionally tell the rich Meccans that they needed to maintain a humble thankfulness, but he did not rebuke them harshly. He simply left them alone. It was because of this that many were tolerant toward this new religion, despite the open hostility of a few. It simply praised God and left outsiders alone. Christians and Jews were actually sympathetic to this message, due to their shared belief in The One God. Muhammad never asked either group to convert to Islam, because they had their own versions of the one religion.

It wasn't until after Muhammad's third year of preaching that he actively spoke out against people worshipping idols. The response from the Meccan community was loud and immediate. No one was willing to abandon the beliefs and idols of their forefathers. Muhammad and all his followers became despised overnight.

Even as the resentment of the community was growing, Muhammad continued to criticize idol and money worship. He even stated that every person would be accountable for their own lives *after* they died. When Muhammad started emphasizing the concept of charity, the Meccans thought it was self-serving and a money grab. Lastly, being told to become humble "servants" of Allah was just too much. In 616 C.E., Muslims were physically attacked by some of the Meccans. A couple of appeals for peace were made from both sides, but the persecution continued. At this point, only Abu Talib, Muhammad's chieftain uncle, stood in the way of the Meccans.

The open animosity split families and led to open fighting. Muhammad and his followers found themselves besieged in the city's Quraish district. Since a good number of the Muslims were poor, the boycott caused some of them to die of starvation. Muhammad, in particular, became a target for ridicule and physical attacks from the populace. While this was troubling for him, it was the treatment of his followers that concerned him more. As things were building to a head, Muhammad got the worst news imaginable: in 619, his beloved wife, Kadeeja, died. Even as he mourned her death, the threat from the Meccans grew. Sensing his weakness, they banded together and moved to drive him from the city. It was at this bleak moment, in the same year, his only defender, his influential uncle, Abu Talib, died.

As the situation deteriorated, Muhammad was approached by a group of people from the nearby settlement of Yathrib. Yathrib was less a city than a patchwork of villages, about twenty of which were comprised of people of the Jewish faith. Jewish prophecies foretold a messenger would come to the Arab people, and some believed Muhammad could be that messenger. This was important because the tribes of Yathrib had begun a slide into civil war, and there was desperate need for an arbitrator who was honorable. If he was divinely guided, all the better. After hearing Muhammad speak in Mecca, the small group from Yathrib decided to invite Muhammad and his followers to arbitrate their dispute.

Given the deteriorating situation in Mecca, Muhammad knew he had no choice but to leave his home town and go to Yathrib. The situation in Mecca had become so bad that people were actually losing their lives now. The problem was that leaving their tribe would further brand them as traitors. Muhammad did not mind this for himself, but worried about his followers who would not only have to leave their homes, but in some cases, their families behind. Nevertheless, as instances of torture and death grew, Muhammad had no choice.

In 622 A.D., Muhammad's followers slowly started to trickle out of Mecca in order to prevent raising an alarm. When the Meccans realized what was happening, they decided Muhammad had crossed the line. They quietly plotted to kill him in his sleep. Some Muslims overheard the plot and spirited Muhammad away before it could be carried out. That night, he and his friend Abu Bakr[2]

---

2. As a personal and political bond, Abu Bakr promised that when his daughter,

attempted to make their way to Yathrib, with the Meccans in hot pursuit. It took them several weeks to arrive.

Muhammad understood that he needed to unite the different districts of the city quickly. First, he made his religious message of equality, humility and empathy clear. He then actively made sure that both the Muslims of Mecca who had migrated with him and the residents of Yathrib thought of each other as brothers and sisters, rather than different factions. This strategy ended up working well and earned Muhammad an even better reputation. The people of Yathrib even renamed the city "Medina" as a symbol of the change that was occurring. Medina literally means "city" but is short for "City of the Prophet."

Muhammad slowly instituted more concepts that promoted charity and good works among the citizens of Medina, which engendered better relations amongst the hamlets. While the integration was working for the Muslims, it was not for others. Only a minority of the Jewish tribes had allied with the Muslims. The largest of these saw their influence declining and decided to join the pagan Arabs in an effort to combat Muslim influence in their city.

Meanwhile, the Meccans were still furious over Muham-

Aisha, was of age she would marry the prophet. Some traditions state she was betrothed at nine and consummated when she was older. A few others state the marriage was consummated when she was nine. None are certain. Some scholars even say that Aisha was nineteen when she was married, [see Maulana Muhammad Ali, "Muhammad, the Prophet and Living Thoughts of the Prophet Muhammad" and Ruqaiyyah Waris Maqsood, "Hazrat Aishah, A Study of Her Age at the Time of Her Marriage" *Islamic Review* (December 1980).] Ultimately, marriage at these ages was common at the time partly because life expectancy was shorter. For instance, Mary, the mother of Jesus, has been claimed to have been around twelve when she was pregnant.

mad's escape, and vowed vengeance. They officially declared war on the tiny Muslim community, promising that they would not show any willingness to reconcile. As soon as Muhammad heard about the declaration of war, he knew it could mean the end for his little community. He needed to find a way to strengthen his people and show the Meccans that they would not stand idly by while they plotted the Muslims' demise. To make matters worse, the Muslims of Medina were suffering monetarily following their emigration due to the lack of available work. The solution was simple: Meccan caravans continually carried goods to Syria. Since a war had already been declared on the Muslims, these caravans became fair game. Appropriating their goods would provide much needed financial relief and show the Meccans they were not afraid of confrontation.

The first two years of raids netted little. It wasn't until the third year that the Muslims began having some success. After a particularly successful caravan raid near a town called Naklah, the Muslims were emboldened and decided to capture the largest caravan of the year. In March 624, Muhammad and his followers set out to ambush it. The Meccans quickly got word of the imminent attack and were incensed at Muhammad's audacity. Abu Lahab, Muhammad's loudest critic, decided to send out a large army to crush the Muslim upstarts once and for all. Even some of Muhammad's own family rode out to meet him in battle.

Ultimately, Abu Lahab sent 1,000 men with one hundred horses. His intention was to send a force so overwhelming that the Muslims would be compelled to surrender without a battle. What neither side knew at the time was that this would actually be the beginning of a larger, more violent war.

The Meccan army camped near the well of Badr in order to display their full strength to the nearby Muslims. The display had the desired effect — the Muslims were terrified. They only had 314 men and two horses. Muhammad gathered his men to consult with them, as he did not make unilateral decisions when lives were on the line. Most showed little confidence in their ability to win against the superior army, but a majority still decided they could not turn back now.

The two armies stood at a stalemate for two days. Obeying a Quranic revelation, Muhammad refused to engage the army until the enemy physically attacked [3]. Instead, they stood resolute and refused to surrender. This enraged the Meccan general, Abu Jahl, who finally decided to attack.

When the Meccans finally did engage the small Muslim army, they were taken aback by the Muslims' determination. The Muslims fought fiercely because they knew if they lost this battle, it would effectively mean an end to Islam and their prophet, Muhammad. This determination proved to be the winning factor. The Meccans, after suffering many losses in the battle, retreated to Mecca.

In the end, the Meccans had lost seventy men, while another seventy had been captured. The Muslims had lost only fourteen.

In addition to the victory, the battle was significant in other ways. The Arab custom at the time was to torture the captured, and mutilate the dead bodies. Muhammad put a permanent stop to this practice by reminding his followers that God forbade it (47:4). It was critical that one show mercy and kindness at all

---

3. This would become the directive for all Muslims for the rest of time.

times. According to the Quran, Muhammad told them his followers should fight to a quick resolution if forced to, but if the enemy ceased and asked for peace, they must comply (2:193). Even in battle, God's commandments applied. This was not always popular with the followers at the time, as they had previously clung to a very different set of ideas and customs. Still, Muhammad was always sure to introduce change slowly in an attempt to give people time to adjust.

The Battle of Badr, as it was called, was an enormous political victory as well. It solidified Muhammad's position in Medina and showed the Meccans that the Muslims were a formidable force. Muhammad's next step was to have a constitution drawn up for Medina. This document gave everyone religious freedom but also insisted that all the tribes must defend Medina against any assault. The agreement was signed by all parties in residence.

At this time, Muhammad married Hafsah, a woman who had been widowed and had not found another husband. Her father, Uthman, was one of Muhammad's closest advisors, and the marriage solidified their professional relationship, while providing Hafsah a stability that widows could not typically find at the time.

For a short time, the Muslim community was able to address family and business life. Muhammad purposely allowed people to see him sewing his own clothes, cobbling his shoes, and tending to livestock. He encouraged his wife Aisha, who was highly intelligent, to begin engaging in Islamic scholarship. As a result, she constantly challenged and debated him in public. This was shocking at the time because women were not supposed to challenge their husbands — privately or publicly. Muhammad encouraged this public display to show that women's opinions were valuable and valid. This did not sit well with the Meccan men that were in Medina, as their own wives were starting to emulate Aisha. Muhammad's tolerance and Aisha's forthrightness had the effect of empowering women to express their opinions and challenge their husbands. As dedicated as these men were to Islam, their clannish egos did not appreciate the interference in their personal lives.

As the short lull continued, Muhammad counseled people who had problems or questions. He also took the time to teach his followers about the religion of God, which was based on mercy and kindness towards family and neighbors—a philosophy that was intended to permeate all aspects of life.

Meanwhile, the Quraish tribe in Mecca was still fuming about their loss and had vowed to wipe the Muslims off the face of the earth. This threat was of great concern to the three largest Jewish tribes in Medina and the chief pagan leader, Ibn Ubay. They depended on trade with Mecca and didn't want to continue the fight with them, despite the constitution they had signed.

On March 11, 625 A.D., the Quraish Meccans marched an army of over 3,000 men toward Medina. The Muslims barely managed to get everyone into the city in time. They camped northwest of the city in front of a small mountain called Mount Uhud.

Muhammad wanted to wait out the siege, as it was next to impossible for any army to camp in the desert for long. He believed in consultation, however, and took a vote. He found that the majority, especially the younger Muslims, wanted to fight. They were bolstered by the victory at Badr, and felt they had the numbers to challenge the Meccans. Muhammad had no choice but to acquiesce.

The Jewish tribes of Medina suddenly declared they would not fight, and Ibn Ubay withdrew all his pagan troops from the army the next morning. This left the Muslims with 700 fighters, which meant they were now outnumbered more than four-to-one. Still, they marched out to face the Meccan army.

According to tradition, Muhammad placed fifty archers on a hilltop and told them that no matter what happened, they were to stay there and hold off the opposing army, so it could not reach the Muslim flanks. The tactic was initially successful, but as the archers watched the Meccans fall, they realized that there was plenty of booty to be recovered. Forty of them charged off the mountain to claim the spoils. The Meccans realized this and cut into the Muslim flanks. Muhammad found himself cut off from all but twenty of his followers and surrounded with only twenty people to defend him— one of whom was a woman. Though they fought hard, the defenders fell one by one as the Meccans closed in. If the Meccans had decided to follow this charge with another, it would have destroyed the Muslims, but they hesitated, giving Muslim reinforcements a chance to stave off any more attacks.

Nonetheless, the Muslims came back to Medina defeated. Sixty-five of their warriors had died, leaving behind at least as many widows and orphans. Given Arab law, these families were doomed because the widows had no right to inherit anything. These women and children would starve without care. It was at this time that Muhammad revealed the following Quranic passage:

> Hence, render unto the orphans their possessions, and do not substitute bad things [of your own] for the good things [that belong to them], and do not consume their possessions together with your own: this, verily, is a great

crime. And if you have reason to fear that you might not act equitably towards orphans, then marry from among [other] women such as are lawful to you —[even] two, or three, or four: but if you have reason to fear that you might not be able to treat them with equal fairness, then [only] one (4:2–3) . . .

This edict was groundbreaking at the time because neither orphans nor women were allowed to even own property. The men in the family would simply take a widow's inheritance and administer it the way they saw fit. The women could then be abused by their male guardians, or even sold into slavery. At this moment, the Quran gave women a legal status that women in Europe would not see for another 900 years[4].

The edict was not well received by many of the Muslims, including some of Muhammad's closest companions. Nonetheless, Muhammad continued his mission to improve the status of women for the rest of his life.

Muhammad had now married two widows, Hafsah and Umm Salamah, in addition to Aisha. These women were becoming major voices in the Islamic community and had started to push Muhammad to better represent women in the community. Muhammad recited a verse from the Quran that addressed both men and women equally (33:35). Soon after that, an entire chapter (*sura*) was dedicated to women (4:1) [5]. Women were no longer to be

---

4. The Book of Numbers in the Bible only allowed daughters to inherit if there were no sons. If there were five daughters and one son, the son would receive the entire inheritance.

5. The Quran was not revealed in the order it exists in now.

bequeathed to men like livestock. They could inherit property and wealth. No woman could be forced into a marriage. Before the Quranic verses were revealed, the groom gave money to a male relative of the bride, who would keep it for himself. Now, the woman was to be given the dowry and it was hers to keep, untouchable by others.

The Muslim men were infuriated. Fighting in battle was one thing, but intrusion into their personal lives was another. They could not understand how someone who did not work or support a family could inherit property. There was one area where men did find a loophole to exploit—domestic abuse. The Quran absolutely condemned violence of men against one another, but men saw violence towards women as "different." Muhammad loathed the concept of beating one's wife and preached against it (Al-Bukhari, vol. 8, Hadith 68). However, men were able to find a Quranic verse [6] that seemed to allow it:

> . . . And as for those women whose ill-will you have reason to fear, admonish them [first]; then leave them alone in bed; then beat [*daraba*] them; and if thereupon they pay you heed, do not seek to harm them (4:34) . . .

The problem was that the Arabic word *daraba* could mean several things. It could mean to reproach one physically or "beat," but it could also simply mean "to leave," in which case, a verbal admonishment by the man would be followed by his leaving the house entirely. To this day, the meaning of the word *daraba* is de-

---

6. These verses were revealed around the end of A.H 3 or A.H. 4, or the beginning of A.H. 5.

bated. The only verifiably authentic tradition Muslims have states that Muhammad taught that physical restraint could only be used if adultery was about to be performed, but "in such a way as not to cause pain" (*ghayr mubarrih*), which negates any form of beating. There is no evidence that Muhammad ever physically or verbally abused any woman in his life.

Regardless, it was a terrible time for Muhammad to convey pro-women edicts. Not only were many Muslims uneasy about all these changes, there was a tremendous amount of political pressure from the tribes of Medina to oust the new Muslims who had drawn the ire of Mecca. As Muhammad's own community was disagreeing more and more about different political and social matters, the Meccans decided to mount another attack.

In March 627, the Meccans approached Medina with a massive 10,000-man army. The Muslims had only about 3,000. The younger men did not jump at the chance to fight this time. A Persian convert to Islam, Salman al-Farsi, suggested a radical strategy that could help them. He proposed they dig a trench around the entire city so it would be difficult to penetrate. This was a new concept to the Arabs, who were less accustomed to siege warfare than the Persians, and even saw it as cowardly to not face your enemy in open combat.

Nevertheless, Muhammad agreed to the plan and somehow managed to motivate his people at this tense time. Crews set about digging the large trench. Muhammad worked alongside them. But the good spirits turned to fear as the Meccan army approached the city and tightened its noose.

After several days, the siege had put a great amount of strain on the city's resources. People started to complain. One Jewish tribe, called the Qurayzah, was one of the most vocal and openly hostile to Muhammad. In an act of defiance, they started sending weapons and supplies to the Meccans despite the treaty they had agreed to with the other tribes of Medina. They even went so far as to mount an attack against the Muslims inside the city, but they could not sustain it. It was treason in every sense of the word.

The siege went on for three weeks. The Quran referred to this point in time:

> [Remember what you felt] when they came upon you from above you and from below you, and when [your] eyes became dim and [your] hearts came up to [your] throats, and [when] most conflicting thoughts about God passed through your minds: [for] there and then were the believers tried, and shaken with a shock severe (33:10–33:11).

Unbeknownst to the Muslims, the Meccan army was having troubles of its own. Their supplies were running thin. The Meccan chief, Abu Sufyan, knew things were not looking good. The final straw came when a giant rainstorm flooded the Meccan camps and destroyed their remaining supplies. They were forced to leave the field and give victory to the Muslims.

Nonetheless, the siege had left some within Medina with growing doubts. Tensions in the city had grown to a fever pitch, and as in Mecca, the city was moving towards civil war. The pagan tribes in particular were certain that the Meccans would return and wipe them out completely. Then there were the traitors, the Qurayzah. They had not only supplied the Meccan army, but had attacked the Muslims during the war. To help calm things down,

Muhammad sent the Qurayzah's former ally, Sad ibn Muadh, to arbitrate. After weighing the consequences, he realized that they were too much of a threat. Breaking a protection law in a written constitution was treason, and the penalty for treason was execution. Since this was the traditional penalty throughout Arabia, the Qurayzah accepted their fate. The women and children would be spared, but 700 men were executed.

Muhammad did not like this sort of violence and killing, but he had no choice but to relent to the arbitrator's decision of execution. The Bedouins and other tribes were waiting to see how their constitution would be enforced and how their own possible actions would be dealt with. With Muhammad's acquiescence, the arbitrator gave the order for execution.

It's important to note that Muhammad did not have any prejudice toward the Jewish tribes at the time. He had befriended seventeen other Jewish tribes in Medina, and none of them made any protest about the execution or his position in their community. This relatively positive relationship between Islam and Judaism would be an important feature of life in Muslim lands up until the conflicts arising out of the Middle Eastern settlement at the end of the First and Second World Wars. As previously mentioned, Muhammad took a positive view of the Christian and Jewish revelations and acknowledged the theological debt owed to them, even if he saw his own as penultimate.

The Battle of the Trench, as it came to be known, was seen as a great victory all over the Arabian Peninsula. More alliances were formed, while hostile parties were challenged. Although the Muslims were seen increasingly favorably everywhere, Medina itself still had quarreling factions. Muhammad maintained some measure of control, but the situation remained tenuous.

Despite the turmoil, Muhammad announced something that no one could have predicted. He would go to the temple of Mecca to perform the Hajj, an annual pilgrimage that was common in Arabia at the time; both before and after Muhammad. Obviously, taking this step was problematic for several reasons. The war between Medina and Mecca was still ongoing, and the Meccans had not softened their opinion of his movement. Compounding this, pilgrims were not allowed to carry weapons. Third, Medina was already turning on itself, and leaving it could be disastrous. Nonetheless, Muhammad insisted he would go on the pilgrimage and asked his followers to accompany him.

The Muslims were uneasy but did have the small consolation that all pilgrims were supposed to be protected by the Meccans. Still, they were taking a huge risk in the wake of their defeat of the Meccan tribes following the Battle of the Trench. In March 628, Muhammad and 1,000 Muslim men and women set out for Mecca with absolutely no weapons.

Bedouins from around Arabia either joined the group or watched from afar as the Muslims reached Mecca. Everyone wanted to know what would happen. Rather than approach the city directly, the Muslims simply rested in a place called *Hudaybiyyah* and waited to hear from Mecca. This was to show they had no intention of fighting. It was, in effect, the first "sit-in." Having received word of what was happening, the Meccans sent General Khalid bin Walid to massacre the Muslims with 200 cavalry. The Meccans were determined to be done with Muhammad. However, violence in *Hudaybiyyah* was a grave taboo, and Walid refused to attack directly: killing the pilgrims was one thing, but doing so inside this area was absolute sacrilege.

After much discussion and a few bluffs, the Meccans decided it would be best to strike a deal with Muhammad. Following prolonged negotiations however, the Muslims found themselves somewhat dismayed at the outcome. Muhammad had agreed to return to Medina without visiting the holy temple, but would be allowed to return the next year. He was also able to negotiate a truce between Mecca and Medina that was to last ten years.

The Muslims were dismayed because they would no longer be able to raid Meccan caravans going to Syria. This would be a serious loss of money—and all the profit would go back to the Meccans. All of this, and the Mulims would not even be able to visit the temple. This was a lot to swallow for an aggressive culture that counted honor and dignity as high virtues. But Muhammad reminded his followers of the Quran's edict to accept peace when offered, and the treaty with Mecca had to be accepted, even if it was not to their complete advantage. This did not satisfy many as the problems would only grow when they returned to Medina, where their position was already tenuous.

Amazingly, as word of the treaty spread, people were impressed with the show of non-violence. Without lifting a sword, the Muslims were able to strike a ten-year truce with the heralded Meccan society. Given the attitudes prevalent at the time, this only increased the mystique surrounding Muhammad and his people. In the next two years, the Muslims more than doubled their population with converts.

Medina, as usual, was still plagued by infighting. Muhammad decided to lay siege to the Jewish clan of Nadir in the nearby city of Khaybar, as the residents had been launching attacks against the Muslims for some time. The siege was successful, and the city surrendered. The success of the siege in Khaybar helped things in Medina, as a major threat had been vanquished. Muhammad took the clan chief's daughter, Safeeya, as his wife to join the clans together. Marrying a Jewish woman was yet another symbol of reconciliation that Muhammad felt was important.

By the end of his life, Muhammad would marry a total of nine women, including his first love, Kadeeja. All of these, except his marriage to Kadeeja, were for either political or compassionate reasons. Most were widows of martyrs and purely political. This was customary at the time in order to bind two groups or families together in an alliance. There have been cries that Muhammad married these women for carnal reasons. However, this would not really make sense. In the prime of his life, at age twenty-five, he married a woman fifteen years his senior and remained monogamous with her for twenty-four years until her death[7]. The more likely scenario is that Muhammad's marriages were principally political.

In March of 629 C.E., more than 2,600 Muslims from Medina set out on what became known as the first pilgrimage to Mecca (the *Umrah Dhu'l Qada*). Part of the Hudaybiyyah treaty provided that the Meccan elders had to leave the city once the Muslims arrived. They did exactly this, and the Muslims marched into the city with quiet resolve. One of Muhammad's closest companions, a black ex-slave named Bilal, stood on the Meccan walls and called the Muslims to prayer by saying "God is greatest. God is greatest." Pronouncing this loudly over the idols had a demoralizing effect on the pagans, as they were forced to watch the Muslims perform

---

7. As a side note, Muhammad and Kadeeja's daughter was the only child of Muhammad alive at the time of his death. Several of his children had died in childbirth or as young children.

their rites, powerless to do anything.

News of the Muslims' pilgrimage spread across Arabia, and more people flocked to Medina to talk to the Muslims and pledge their allegiance. To the Muslims' great surprise, even the pagan Meccan general, Khalid bin Walid, converted. He did so with considerable trepidation, as he had been responsible for numerous Muslim deaths. Nevertheless, Muhammad reminded him and all others that all sins were forgiven upon entering Islam. Khalid bin Walid would go on to become one of the greatest Muslim generals of all time, playing a key role in subduing the Arabian Peninsula and in the wars against the Persians.

In November of that same year, the Quraish Meccans broke the treaty of Hudaybiyyah by attacking a Muslim ally. The Muslims had grown tremendously in number and could now overpower them. Too late, the Meccans realized they had made a terrible mistake. Muhammad also realized this, and in January of 630 set out for Mecca with 10,000 men.

Before they reached Mecca, Abu Sufyan, the Meccan leader, set out to talk to Muhammad. Abu Sufyan said that he now believed in Allah, as he had watched all the miraculous victories and growth that had occurred in the preceding years. However, he was not ready to accept that Muhammad was the prophet. Muhammad accepted this and told him that anyone who put himself under his protection would be safe. Before leaving, Abu Sufyan was astounded to see all the Muslims bowing down in prayer in unison. At such a display of collective will, he told the people of Mecca that defeat was inevitable.

The Muslims then walked into Mecca without shedding a single drop of blood. The Meccans feared the inevitable slaughter that would occur, but Muhammad declared that everyone was to be given amnesty and that no one would be pressured to convert to Islam.

Muhammad solemnly walked into the temple, or Kaaba, and started destroying the idols, one by one. It was said that the only things he allowed to remain were frescoes of Jesus and Mary. Muhammad reminded everyone that the Kaaba had originally been built by Abraham and Ishmael together, and it was a place dedicated to al-Lah, the one God. Muhammad then called out to the people of the Quraish tribe a verse from the Quran:

> O men! Behold, We have created you all out of a male and a female, and have made you into nations and tribes, so that you might come to know one another. Verily, the noblest of you in the sight of God is the one who is most deeply conscious of Him. Behold, God is all-knowing, all-aware (49:13).

The people of Mecca finally came out of their houses and began either to ask for forgiveness, or to swear fealty to the new leader. Muhammad's greatest enemies were not only promoted in the city's government, but were adorned with gifts as well.

Upon returning to Medina, Muhammad found that most of Arabia was ready to accept his leadership, if not his religion. In ten years, Muhammad had changed the entire landscape of Arabia, and become the leader of a land that had been filled with thousands of warring tribes and religions.

However, in the beginning of 632, Muhammad's health was failing. He made plans to take what many thought would be his last pilgrimage to Mecca. At the end of the rituals, Muhammad stood on Mount Arafat in front of a crowd of 140,000 and gave what become known as his final sermon to his people. He took particular care to address kindness to women, and to emphasize that peace and unity were critical to a Muslim's life. Of brotherhood and equality, he said:

All mankind is from Adam and Eve; an Arab has no superiority over a non-Arab nor a non-Arab has any superiority over an Arab; also a white has no superiority over black nor a black has any superiority over white except by piety and good action. Learn that every Muslim is a brother to every Muslim and that the Muslims constitute one brotherhood. Nothing shall be legitimate to a Muslim which belongs to a fellow Muslim unless it was given freely and willingly. Do not, therefore, do injustice to yourselves (Al-Bukhari, Hadith 1623, 1626, 6361).

When Muhammad returned to Medina, he started having severe headaches and fainting spells. He asked his best friend, Abu Bakr, to lead the prayers as he listened quietly beside him. People seemed in denial, as they could not contemplate losing their prophet and leader. Moreover, people were worried the religion would die and with it, the community that had been built.

One afternoon, Muhammad's wife, Aisha, felt him leaning on her more heavily than usual. He then laid his head in her lap and passed away in her arms.

Abu Bakr heard the cries of mourning as he came near to Muhammad's house and instantly knew what had happened. A stunned crowd had gathered and was listening to one of Muhammad's closest friends, Umar. Umar was telling everyone that Muhammad had only left for a little while and would return. Abu Bakr calmly took the stage and corrected the emotional Umar. He said, "O people, if anyone worships Muhammad, Muhammad is dead." He paused for a second. "If anyone worships God, God is alive, immortal." He added that to deny Muhammad's death was to deny his message. Muhammad was still only a mortal and, therefore, one of them. He must not be worshipped or venerated beyond his status as the prophet of God. Abu Bakr then recited a verse from the Quran that addressed a time at Uhud when everyone thought Muhammad had died in battle:

And Muhammad is only an apostle; all the [other] apostles have passed away before him: if, then, he dies or is slain, will you turn about on your heels? But he that turns about on his heels can in no way harm God—whereas God will requite all who are grateful [to Him]. (3:144)

After some time had passed, Umar nominated Abu Bakr as the new leader, or first Caliph, of the Muslim community. A majority concurred, though there was a minority who believed that his nephew, Ali ibn Abi Talib, should have been the next leader. In later years, this minority sect would later become known as the Shiites, and the followers of Abu Bakr would become the Sunni. Ali eventually did become leader of the Muslims, but only after two of the prophet's companions had done so. With all the infighting, no Muslim could have predicted that within fifty years, Islam would spread to three different continents.

Some of Muhammad's critics, and even some Muslim scholars, believe His wars against the pagans were one of His greatest accomplishments. A quick review of his life, however, shows that He regarded the wars as defensive wars and more of a necessary evil. He spent more time preaching against the cyclical nature of violence and dedicated the majority of his life to compassion and peace. This was evident in his final conquest of Mecca in which he did not spill a drop of blood. He was to his end, a champion of nonviolence even in the most perilous of times.

As a testament to his life and teachings, Abu Bakr collected the acts and words of the prophet into a single book. The resulting book, called the Quran, is still considered the greatest of Muhammad's acts — a miracle in fact. The most amazing thing to the early Muslims was the actual language of the Quran. The beauty of its language was unparalleled while its message was complex and meaningful. It was considered to be a miracle within itself. Early historical accounts state that some people converted to Islam right after only hearing several paragraphs of the revelation. This is why, to this day, Muslims consider the Arabic of the Quran—and not translations—the best way to read and receive the full meaning of its text.

Muhammad had accomplished in twenty years what many thought was impossible, and would go on, to unite all the various tribes of Arabia and introduce what many described as "the one religion," a religion that now has more than 1.6 billion followers. His life and His accomplishments were made all the greater by His commitment to justice and fraternity. His people would go on to change the course of history in uncountable ways and regardless of religious conviction; one cannot doubt the debt posterity owes to the acts of this man.

CONCLUSION

Islam, at its core, is a simple religion. The five basic pillars, the Quran and Muhammad's life are really what comprise the entirety of the religion.

Like any religion, it can be interpreted and practiced in different ways, ranging from very liberal to very strict adherence. Speaking to this point, Muhammad said to one of his companions: "Make things easy for the people [in matters of religion] and do not put hurdles in their way, and give them glad tidings. . . (B 009.089.284)"

It is not adherence that can cause problems for Islam; it's misinterpretation by some of its followers. This can and has bred extremism. While Islamic extremists constitute a tiny minority, they do attract the most publicity. Their actions are not an accurate representation of most of Islam's 1.6 billion followers, who do practice Islam correctly and in a peaceful way.

Another problem for Muslims today is the lack of education in the countries they call home. This has led to an adherence to older cultural traditions and superstitions that should have nothing to do with Islam. Some of these holdovers include sexism, violence, and bigotry. The governments in these countries, most of which are oppressive dictatorships or monarchies, have little interest in educating their people, since Islam forbids oppression and could undermine their authority. This lack of education in the Islamic world is regrettable considering that the last time Muslims embraced learning and scholarship, it led to an era that birthed modern science, medicine, and art.

Everyone does not view Islam favorably however, and a great deal of misinformation is still being spread that seeks to defame Islam. Some do this by taking quotes out of context, redefining words in Arabic, or by using the example of Muslims who practice the faith incorrectly. Such misunderstanding and frauds feed into people's fears and maintain their power because of the fact that few people will do the research themselves.

However, the consequences of fear and ignorance are dire. History has shown these mistakes to result in murder, subjugation, oppression, and war. It's obvious there is much more to be gained by understanding and dialogue, but this cannot happen without factual information and a willingness to explore it. This applies to Muslims and non-Muslims alike.

SELECTED BIBLIOGRAPHY

Al-Hafiz Zakiuddin Abdul-Azim Al-Mundhiri, *Summarized Shahih Muslim*, Darussalam, 2000

An-Nawawi, *Forty Hadith*, Islamic Book Service, New Delhi, India, 2011

Armstrong, Karen. *Muhammad, A Prophet for Our Time.* New York: Harper Collins, 2006.

Asad, Muhammad, *The Message of The Quran*, Muhammad Asad, Dar Al-Andalus, 1980

Hewer, C. T. R. *Understanding Islam: An Introduction.* Minneapolis, MN: Fortress Press, 2006.

Kamal, F., *Easily Understand Islam*, Desert Well Network, 2006

Khan, Muhammad Muhsin, *Summarized Sahih Al-Bukhari,*
   Darussalam, 1994

Lang, Jeffrey, *Struggling to Surrender: Some Impressions of An
   American Convert to Islam.* Beltsville, MD: Amana Publications, 1995.

Lings, Martin. *Muhammad: His Life Based on the Earliest Sources.*
   Vermont: Inner Traditions Press, 2006.

Lippman, Thomas W., *Understanding Islam,* Mentor, 1982

Ramadan, Tariq, *In the Footsteps of the Prophet,* Oxford University
   Press, 2007

Tahir al-Qadri, Muhammad. *The Constitution of Medina.* Lon-
   don: Minhaj-ul-Quran Publications, 2012.

INDEX

H

I

J

Y

Z

ABOUT THE AUTHOR

Tariq Jalil was born and raised in Columbus, Ohio. After graduating from The Ohio State University he went on to work for NBC and Telemundo news, and now resides in Los Angeles, California.

Printed in Great Britain
by Amazon